THE LIVERIES OF THE

PRE-GROUPING RAILWAYS

VOLUME TWO

THE EAST OF ENGLAND AND SCOTLAND

The livery of the Eastern & Midlands Railway, seen here on Class 'B' 4-4-0T No. 20 (formerly *King's Lynn*), had much in common with that of its successor the Midland & Great Northern Joint Railway.

THE LIVERIES OF THE PRE-GROUPING RAILWAYS

VOLUME TWO

THE EAST OF ENGLAND AND SCOTLAND

NIGEL J.L. DIGBY

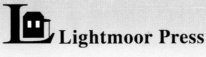
Lightmoor Press

© Nigel J.L. Digby and
Lightmoor Press 2018

Designed by Nigel Nicholson

British Library Cataloguing-in-Publication Data.
A catalogue record for this book is available
from the British Library

ISBN 9781 911038 45 0

LIGHTMOOR PRESS

Unit 144B, Lydney Trading Estate, Harbour Road,
Lydney, Gloucestershire GL15 4EJ

www.lightmoor.co.uk

Lightmoor Press is an imprint of
Black Dwarf Lightmoor Publications Ltd

Printed in Poland; www.lfbookservices.co.uk

The interior of Melton Constable carriage and wagon shop in 1960 when it was still being used for wagon and sheet repairs.
The timber wall on the right was once the exterior wall of the paint shop as extended in 1903.

D.A. Digby

Contents

NOTE TO READERS: Page numbers in this series run consecutively across all four volumes; Volume One is pages 1-96, this volume is pages 97-192 and Volume Three will start on page 193.

Erratum

In Volume One, the background colour of Taff Vale Railway brass numberplates was shown on the painting and in the text as vermilion. This is incorrect, they were black. I knew this, and a simple cross-reference to the chapter on the Rhondda & Swansea Bay Railway would have reminded me to correct it. This I failed to do, for which I can only apologise. My grateful thanks to Cliff Harris for bringing the error to my attention.

Introduction to Volume Two

It is my pleasure to present Volume Two in the series, which deals with railways which were mainly on the eastern side of Great Britain, although some might be considered to have been in the Midlands, such as the Great Central Railway. However, all of the featured railways became part of the London & North Eastern Railway, most from 1923, but the Midland & Great Northern (jointly-owned with the London, Midland & Scottish Railway) from 1936. Not all the members of the L&NER family are here, the Wrexham, Mold & Connah's Quay Railway being in Volume One and the other great L&NER/LM&SR Joint line, the Cheshire Lines Committee, in Volume Three.

Readers must bear in mind that, although my paintings can show small details, my text can only be in the broadest brush strokes. If more particular information is required then I must direct them towards the work of the Historical Model Railway Society and the livery specialists of the other railway societies, upon whom I have relied heavily. Detailed acknowledgements are given as an Appendix in Volume Four. For this volume, further sketches, paintings and contemporary postcards have been added. I have also revised some paintings and their text according to new information received.

Where possible, the colours are given references. The first [Carter] is from the colour chart in E.F. Carter's *Britain's Railway Liveries*. The second reference [Pantone] is from the Pantone PMS formula guide. The third [BS] is from the British Standard colour charts, of which there are several. Occasionally, where there is no close match to these charts, the European RAL standard has been employed. I have not included Munsell references, as it is almost impossible to get physical access to a Munsell chart, whereas the others are readily available to order online. Rather than interrupt the flow of the text, the colour references are shown as footnotes. However, where I have good reason to believe a colour is a match, but have no documentary evidence to prove it, I have mentioned this in the body of the text.

Nigel Digby
Cromer 2018

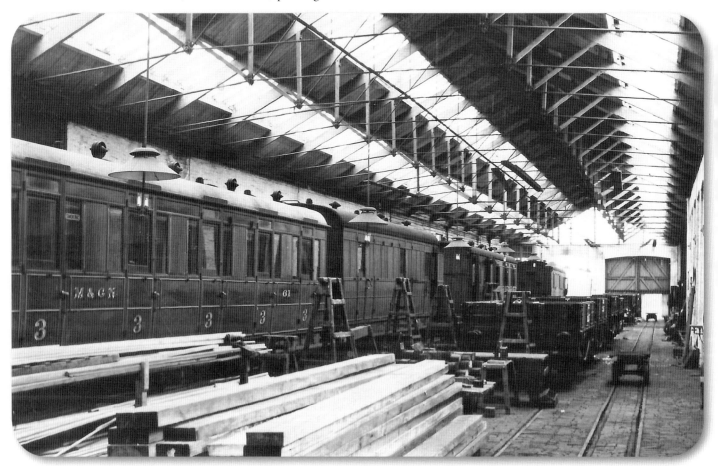

Inside the M&GN's carriage & wagon shop at Melton Constable.

More Materials and Methods

A glossary of the paints, varnishes and methods used in the railway paint shop appears in Volume One. Hopefully this will remind readers that oil paints during the period covered (circa 1890 to circa 1914) behaved very differently from today's single-coat paints, and that painters were a highly-skilled group of men who could not just nip down to the high street for a spray can of the desired colour. To expand on the glossary, I have added here some other materials, names and methods that appear in this volume.

White Pigments

Almost all paint shops used white lead exclusively. This was manufactured from basic lead (II) carbonate, it was also known as flake white and sometimes Cremnitz (or Kremnitz) white.

Yellow Pigments

All yellows other than yellow ochre were manufactured lead chromate, known as chrome yellow. Chrome yellow came in different intensities, from the paler lemon chrome, through middle chrome yellow to the deep orange chrome. Where yellow lining was required, lemon chrome was usually the colour of choice, as the many layers of varnish deepened the colour to a middle chrome. Had middle chrome yellow been used at the start, the lining would appear more orange after varnishing. Sometimes, despite the best efforts of the painters, this happened over time anyway.

Extenders

To make certain transparent paints more opaque and be able to cover greater areas (and also to be a little cheaper), extenders were sometimes used. The usual extender was Barytes, which was mostly natural barium sulphate. This had some body and would inevitably lighten the hue of the paint to which it was being added. Extenders were added to Prussian blue to make Brunswick blue, to which the addition of chrome yellow yielded Brunswick green in a variety of shades.

Buff

This colour appears in the palette of several railways, not least because it was one of the base coats used for the graining of carriages to imitate natural teak. Unusually the Great Eastern Railway preferred it instead of vermilion for painting the motion between the locomotive frames. Many railways used it for the interior of their locomotive cabs. It is usually taken to be a mixture of two parts lead white, with one part yellow ochre. A small amount of burnt sienna or Indian red could sometimes be added if a warmer shade was required. A modern paint equivalent is BS 381 358 Light Buff.

Stone Colour

This was another railway paint that often arrived ready-mixed, like teak colour did. It was a similar colour to buff, but less yellow, and generally taken to be made up from five parts white, two parts yellow ochre and one part burnt umber. A modern paint equivalent is BS 381 361 Light Stone.

Gold

Gold leaf was used for lining, affixed with gold size. The most suitable method for lining rolling stock was ribbon gilding, where a strip of gold leaf was held on a gilding wheel, allowing rapid and economical application. Gold leaf could also be used for lettering, but more frequently transfers of lettering were provided already gilded.

Gold Colour

This was often used for the lining and lettering of secondary stock, and attempted to reproduce the effect of gold in a cheaper way. It was a rich cream or caramel colour made from tinting lead white with a mix of five parts yellow ochre and one part vermilion, and is used by signwriters to this day.

Gold Size

Gold size was a glutinous varnish made with a high proportion of resin and driers, but little linseed oil. It dried quickly to a dull, hard finish, and was used as a sealing coat for teak and as an adhesive for gold leaf. It was often added to oil paint as a drier or siccative to ensure that a coat a day was possible.

Teak

Teak is an oily wood and had to be prepared by applying a sealing coat of gold size. Some panels of the wood may have been lighter than the others, and to ensure a uniform appearance, these would have been stained to match their fellows. Over this preparation were two or three coats of varnish, then lining and lettering, followed by several more coats of varnish, then the finishing varnish.

Teak Colour

This was a reddish brown paint, also known as carriage brown or solebar brown and used to simulate the colour of the varnished wood. From examples I have sampled myself, a modern paint equivalent is BS 318 489 Leaf Brown.

Painting and Graining

Painting and graining was one of the most skilled aspects of the railway paint shop. To simulate teak, over a base of lead colour were applied two or three coats of buff, made richer with a little Indian red to give a deep, pinkish cream. Over this were the graining coats, using various brown water colours bound with stale beer and thinned with rainwater, known as distemper graining. The close graining of teak would have been simulated by drawing graining combs and stiff brushes down the length of the panel, finished off by overgraining with a special brush having separated bristles, then the edges softened with a badger hair brush. A coat of varnish secured the graining before the application of lining and lettering.

BRONZING

Associated with the treatment of varnished teak carriages, and those painted and grained, was the technique of bronzing the ironwork of the body and solebar, and sometimes the iron flitchplate of the entire solebar. After the usual preparation with lead colour, the items to be bronzed were painted dark green. Over this came the application of a special shellac varnish containing metallic bronze powder. To protect the bronzed metal, there followed one or two coats of finishing varnish.

VARNISH

This was invariably an oil-based resin varnish, which possessed its own yellow colour, particularly when applied in several layers, as was the custom. Under these circumstances, whites were turned creamy, greys and blues turned greenish, and pale yellows turned deep yellow, particularly as the varnish became considerably darker with age. Two types were commonly used. The preparatory layers were usually rubbing varnish or body varnish, high in resin and low in oil content, which dried quickly and were rubbed or flatted between coats. On top of this was the finishing varnish, which had a higher proportion of oil and dried more slowly to a high degree of gloss, with great resistance to exposure.

CARRIAGE CONSTRUCTION

There were standard methods of making carriages, and recognised names for each part, as one would imagine. The side of a carriage was usually made up from oak or teak framing. The main vertical members of a typical carriage panel incorporating two windows were the standing pillars, which framed each side of the door openings, and the intermediate pillar halfway between. Filling the gaps were panel battens. The horizontal members were the bottom side, waist rail, bottom light rail, top light rail, and cantrail. The top and bottom light rails supported the windows, more correctly called quarter lights, with the quarter light uprights finishing off the rectangles where the mouldings and glass would be installed.

Over the framing was applied the panelling, of ⅜-inch hardwood, either mahogany or teak, backed with canvas. The panels were sized to fit over the rails beneath, and were pinned and glued onto them with their edges abutting. Covering the joints between each panel was the beading, actually called the fascia, also ⅜ of an inch thick. At the bottom of the side, the finishing strip of beading or fascia was called the shell moulding. The body side was now effectively divided into sectors: the bottom quarter panel, the waist panel, the quarter lights (windows) with the upright panel between them, and the top quarter panel. At the very top, securing the canvas roof covering and acting as a gutter for rainwater, was the cornice.

The Melton Constable carriage and wagon staff posing outside the doors of their shop circa 1910, with an ex-GNR carriage and the rear of an 0-6-0 shunting tank visible inside.

M&GN Circle

Colne Valley & Halstead Railway

On the remote and picturesque border between Essex and Suffolk, a small independent railway managed to survive, despite being surrounded by the giant Great Eastern Railway. The Colne Valley & Halstead Railway obtained its first Act for a line to serve Halstead in 1856. Its eastern junction was with the 1849 Marks Tey to Sudbury branch of the Eastern Counties Railway (from 1862 the GER) at Chappel. Opened to Halstead in 1860, the line was extended over the succeeding years along the Colne Valley, finally opening to Haverhill in 1863. The completed length was 19 miles of single track, much less than the original ambition of building to Cambridge and involving the London & North Western Railway. The GER finished their circuitous Stour Valley line from Sudbury to Cambridge in 1865, with a separate station at Haverhill. However, a link line from the GER to the CV&H at Colne Valley Junction enabled Colne Valley trains to use the GE station, and most of them did so. At the eastern end, Colne Valley coaches could be worked through to the main line at Marks Tey by GER trains.

Being a small line, the amount of stock was limited. In 1909 there were five locomotives, sixteen passenger vehicles and 138 wagons. When first opened, the Colne Valley was worked in a rather individual way under general manager Mr R.J. Watt, resulting in receivership in 1874. In 1877 Mr John Crabtree of the GNR was appointed general manager to replace his incompetent predecessor, and the situation steadily improved. Finances were finally sorted out by an Act of 1885. Mr Crabtree left in 1882 to manage the Great Northern & Great Eastern Joint. The new manager and locomotive

superintendent was Mr George Copus. He was succeeded in 1903 by Mr Elyot S. Hawkins and this gentleman managed the line until Grouping.

The CV&H was absorbed by the London & North Eastern Railway in 1923, and passed to the Eastern Region of British Railways in 1948.

For the first twenty years of the company locomotives were green. Lining appears to have been black with incurved corners, fine-lined in white. The three 2-4-0WT engines were named *Brewster*, *Colne* and *Halstead* with no numbers. The rectangular brass nameplates had the border and the name polished, probably with a vermilion background, and were fixed on the sides of the boiler. When a new 0-4-2T engine arrived in 1876 it was given a number, which it carried on a small elliptical plate on the tankside, having the initials "C.V.R" curving over "Nº 1" in polished brass, again probably with a vermilion background. In about 1880 an ex-Cornwall Minerals Railway 0-6-0T was purchased carrying their No. 10, but the Colne Valley workshops removed the number, painted the engine the standard green, and named it *Haverhill*. It was sold in 1889. An 0-4-2ST engine came from the North London Railway in 1883, and was known as 'No. 2', but never actually carried the number. It was sold in 1894.

In 1887 there arrived two 2-4-2 side tank engines, built by Hawthorn Leslie & Co. They were painted dark crimson, probably similar to the Midland Railway colour [1], with black edging to the panels and lined out in black with incurved corners. The fine-lining is unknown, but was probably vermilion as it registers only

Panel of 2-4-2T Hedingham in original 1894 livery.

faintly on photographs. They carried names *Halstead* and *Colne* in the house style of rectangular brass plate with characters in seriffed capitals. The three old 2-4-0WTs were withdrawn. Another 2-4-2T, *Hedingham*, arrived in 1894. The new colour indicated a change in the company's style, as 0-4-2T No. 1 was also painted crimson when overhauled in 1888. However, this period did not last long, as when No. 1 was rebuilt again at Stratford in 1894 it was turned out in black, apparently lined with a single line of vermilion around the tanks. When the 2-4-2Ts were rebuilt in 1896, 1897 and 1902, they also appeared in black, lined in a similar fashion.

From 1903 Mr Hawkins began smartening up the locomotives, but despite the small number of engines, no real standardisation occurred. The two most uniform in appearance were *Halstead* and *Colne*. They remained black but were given panels of vermilion [2]

lining with incurved corners, fine-lined in white. Boiler bands were vermilion edged in white. Details below the footplate were also picked out in white and vermilion. On either side of the tankside name, the company initials "C V" were placed in large (about 10 inch) gold letters, with a transfer of the heraldic device above.

The engine *Hedingham* had a slightly different livery, possibly applied when rebuilt in 1902. Its lining can still be made out to be a double line, probably on each side of vermilion, but in photographs the outer line is prominent and the inner line is almost invisible. This suggests that the outer line is white but the inner line may be yellow. The engine did receive the large initials, but never seems to have had the device. Engine No. 1 was not repainted and did not have lettering or the device, except "Nº 1" transferred on the rear of the bunker, and of course the original numberplate.

By 1908, numbers had been allocated to the named engines, *Halstead* becoming No. 2, *Colne* No. 3 and *Hedingham* No. 4. Numbers were applied on the bufferbeams in the usual way, for example "Nº [hook] 3", probably in gold characters shaded in black. The bufferbeams were vermilion outlined in black with white fine-lining. Prior to the official numbering, the three engines had allegedly carried their works numbers (Hawthorn, Leslie 2079, 2080 and 2283 respectively) on the bufferbeam, but no photograph showing this appears to exist.

The last new engine to be purchased was 0-6-2T No. 5 in 1908. This carried the black livery, lined in vermilion and white. Its number was transferred onto the bufferbeams, and "Nº 5" also appeared on a small elliptical brass plate just above the centre of the tank. Below this plate, the initials "C V & H R" were spaced

out in small gold sans-serif letters. The heraldic device appeared on the cabside.

During the 1914-18 war, the names were removed and the engine numbers in large brass numerals applied to the bunkers instead. Engines numbered 1 and 5 retained their numberplates. All of the engines became very dirty, but it is still possible to see faint traces of the lining under the dust. The initials and devices seem to have been painted out, except on No. 3, which was given a new transfer of the device centrally on the tanks where the nameplate had once been. This was the state of the locomotive stock when bequeathed to the L&NER in 1923. Three of the CV&HR engines survived to work under their new owners for several years more, No. 2 and No. 3 became L&NER Class 'F9' No. 8312 and No. 8313, and No. 5 became Class 'N18' No. 8314.

Carriage stock was of a mixed nature. The earliest eleven carriages were quite primitive 4-wheelers, but between 1887 and 1899 ten 6-wheel vehicles (four Thirds, one Brake Third, two Composites and three Luggage Brakes) were purchased secondhand from various sources. In the *Railway Year Book* of 1905 there were reported to be fifteen passenger train vehicles, including horseboxes. By studying the Working Timetables, it is clear that the services throughout all the pre-Grouping period could be maintained by two sets, usually of three or four 6-wheel carriages each, and so there were several spares for strengthening or repair. The older 4-wheeled carriages were withdrawn (the body of one appeared as the waiting room at White Colne station), until only two were left for use in trains by 1903.

Carriage livery was described as 'drab'. Despite the modern perception of the word merely as an adjective, drab is an actual colour,

the pale greyish-brown of undyed cloth. However, in this context, it almost certainly refers to a typical plain carriage brown or teak colour. Lining was in black and yellow. Faint traces on photographs suggest that the lining was applied differently according to the type of vehicle. Some of the 6-wheel carriages had no top quarter panels, and an applied rectangle of beading at the waist. Lining was applied around the vertical panels, and on the waist beading, possibly with a central black line. The remainder of the secondhand stock was built by the Metropolitan Carriage & Wagon Co. (which resembled that of the GER) or the Midland Railway, and had conventional beading or fascias. On these vehicles it seems possible that this beading was painted black, then lined with yellow. Although details are scanty, it appears that lettering on all vehicles was "C V R" and the number in the waist. Class marking was a mix of numeral and word, for example "3RD". It is unlikely, despite the arrival of the vehicles noted

below, that the livery of these carriages was changed in the lifetime of the railway.

In 1906 Mr Hawkins purchased three bogie vehicles from the Metropolitan District Railway. These vehicles had been part of a 6-car experimental electric set built by Brown, Marshalls & Co., with electrical equipment by Siemens. Completed in 1899, the set of four trailer cars with two motor-coaches ran between Earl's Court and Kensington (High Street) as a precursor to full electrification. All were 39ft 6ins in length. The 7-compartment bogie Third and 6-compartment bogie Composite required minimal changes, and were delivered to the CV&HR in October 1906. One vehicle had been a motor carriage and required more extensive rebuilding. It was converted into a Brake Third and arrived in April 1908. It is fair to assume that these three carriages became the premier carriage set of the line and, as one set was sufficient for most of the typical

weekday services, would have been used on the bulk of the trains, except when in the workshops for repair or overhaul.

The District stock, consisting of Third No. 11, Composite No. 12 and the converted Brake Third No. 13, arrived in varnished teak and remained so, lined in 'gold' (possibly yellow), following the edges of the body mouldings and the prominent door ventilators. The lettering was in gold, seriffed in GER style, and was shaded, possibly in red, shadowed in black. A shortened version of the company name "COLNE" and "VALLEY" was placed in the eaves panels of the Composite and the Third, where there was room, but in the waist panels of the Brake Third, which had unusual body styling owing to its origins as a motor coach. The running number was placed centrally in the waist in the form "Nº 12", for example. A monogram of the company initials "CVR" was featured on the lower body panels, once beneath the central numbers of the Third

NIGEL J.L. DIGBY 2001

and Brake Third, but twice on the Composite, directly below each word of the company name. Class marking was in numerals slightly larger than the numbers, below the waist of each door.

Goods stock is described in contemporary magazines as being 'French' grey or 'dull grey', but photographs show merely a light medium grey, and common sense and a consideration of paint shop practices would suggest a simple standard lead colour. Below the solebar was black.

By the 1890s it seems that the initials "C.V.R" were being used, in small letters similar to the GER style. However, during the early years of the 20th century the initials "C V" appeared in large white characters with bold serifs, between 12 and 18 inches high, depending on wagon. A partial view of a van implies that some stock had unseriffed letters. The number was painted to the lower left of the sides of open wagons in a seriffed style, and also on the wagon ends. Brake vans apparently kept the earlier lettering, having "C.V.R." centrally with the number below, for example "Nº 8", all in white characters about 6 inches high.

1 'CRIMSON'
CARTER 28
PANTONE 188
BS 381 540 'CRIMSON'

2 'VERMILION'
CARTER 36
PANTONE 485
BS 5252 04 E 55
OR BS 381 536
'POPPY RED'

Great Central Railway

The Manchester, Sheffield & Lincolnshire Railway (p. 155) was formed by amalgamation in 1847, and had a compact system serving Manchester, Sheffield, Doncaster, Grimsby and Lincoln. The Chairman of the MS&LR, Sir Edward Watkin, pressed for a line to the capital, and after much opposition the London Extension was completed in 1899. To complement its new status as a trunk line, the MS&LR was renamed the Great Central Railway in 1897.

The London Extension made its way through Nottingham and Leicester to join the Metropolitan Railway at Quainton Road. Once in London, the GCR line left the Metropolitan alignment and ran into a new terminus at Marylebone. The shared line became the Metropolitan & Great Central Joint in 1906, at the same time as a joint line with the Great Western was opened through Princes Risborough. The GCR continued to expand throughout the decade. The Wrexham, Mold & Connah's Quay Railway (see Volume One) was absorbed in 1905, followed by the Lancashire, Derbyshire & East Coast (p. 149) in 1907. A new concentration yard at Wath-upon-Dearne was opened and several new joint lines were constructed in South Yorkshire. The GCR also developed a new port at Immingham.

The Great Central Railway became a constituent of the London & North Eastern Railway in 1923 and passed to the Eastern Region of British Railways in 1948. However, under an exchange scheme in 1958, the main line to London was transferred to the London Midland Region.

In 1897 the Locomotive Superintendent was Mr H. Pollitt, who continued the MS&LR livery of light chrome green and brown, lined in black and yellow, except that the lettering was now "GREAT CENTRAL". Numbers were on cabs or bunkers in gold transfers, shaded in red. The new coat of arms (one of the few actually registered with the College of Heralds) appeared on the splashers of express locomotives. It consisted of a shield carrying the arms of Manchester, Sheffield and Lincoln over the arms of the City of London. The crest was a winged locomotive and below the shield was the motto "FORWARD". This motto was also adopted by the GCR's successor, the L&NER, in 1923.

Mr Pollitt was succeeded in 1900 by Mr J.G. Robinson. The first signs of a new livery scheme were seen in September 1901, on the appearance of the Class '9J' 0-6-0s which were black, but Mr Robinson's first passenger engines (the Class '11B' 4-4-0s of 1901-3) retained a version of the Pollitt livery, lined in black and

Class '1' 4-6-0 No. 423 *Sir Sam Fay* as new in December 1912. This rendition of the livery shows the vermilion fine lining on the tender, cab and crimson areas to good effect, but the upper lining on the bufferbeam is not correct. Three of the class of six were painted in the black livery. *Author's collection*

yellow. However, the lining style was new, the broad black borders used formerly now being reduced to a narrow edging, and bands of lining appearing on the tenders. Lettering of both new classes was "GREAT [arms] CENTRAL" and the coat of arms appeared again on the driving-wheel splashers of the 4-4-0s. By the Spring of 1903 the new liveries were evident; passenger classes were to be painted dark green and mixed traffic and goods types were to be black.

The painting specifications issued for Robinson engines called for thorough surface preparation of the entire engine and tender, which included two coats of lead colour with filling and stopping. The whole locomotive was then painted two coats of lead colour, except between the frames and on the bufferbeams, which received a coat of flesh colour as a base for the vermilion which would be applied there.

Passenger engines were specified to be painted Brunswick green [1], a medium-dark chrome green, manufactured from Brunswick blue and chrome yellow. It is said that the green had a slight 'olive' cast to it. Two coats of Brunswick green were applied to the lead colour undercoat on boiler and firebox clothing, cabs, wheels, tanks and tenders. Originally all wheel splashers were also painted green, and this continued for most classes, but there were notable exceptions (see below).

A contrast colour was adopted for green engines, which was specified as crimson lake [2]. It is possible that the crimson was either alizarin or carmine, which were similar, and both transparent, but had different behaviours after application. However, what really made the final colour different from that of Midland Railway engines (Volume Three) was that the two coats of crimson lake were applied to the grey undercoat. Midland engines employed a red-brown undercoat, which tended to strengthen the red of the crimson, whereas grey would mute the red and add blue undertones, leading some commentators to call it purple brown, or claret. Outside frames, main frames above the footplate, valancing, outside cylinders, step irons and buffer casings were all crimson lake.

It is believed that the 1905 batch of Class '8B' 4-4-2s (the 'Jersey Lillies') were the first engines to have crimson splashers, and eventually all the Atlantics had them. This new tendency led to the adoption of crimson for the continuous splashers of the green Class '1' 4-6-0s (the 'Sam Fays') and the 4-cylinder Class '9P' 4-6-0s (the 'Lord Faringdons').

Main frames, cab roofs, smokeboxes, step treads, footplates, and fronts and tops of tenders were black, although the Class '11E'/'11F' 4-4-0s and the Class '9P' 4-6-0s had crimson tender

NIGEL J. L. DIGBY 1999

fronts. Inside faces of main frames, motion and buffer beams had two coats of vermilion [3]. Cab interiors had received only one coat of lead colour in the preparation phase and were finished stone colour. Handrails, coupling rods and other similar items were polished metal. Bufferbeams were edged in black and fine-lined in white except along the top edge. Buffer casings were lined in black and white at base and lip.

Body panels were edged in black, with a fine line between the black and panel colour, which varied according to type and position. All tender locomotives had vermilion fine-lining on the crimson areas and around the tender panels, and this also occurred on the cab sides of locomotives with cabs separate from driving wheel splashers (4-2-2s, 4-4-2s and 4-6-0s). Green splashers were fine-lined in white, and where cabs were part of the same panel (as on most 4-4-0s) the white fine-lining was continued onto them. Upon the green body panels of all engines were broad bands of black lining with normal curved corners, fine-lined with white. Boiler bands were also black, edged with white.

Tank locomotives differed from the tender locomotives in that all fine-lining was in white, including on crimson panels. Only the Class '9N' 4-6-2Ts retained the vermilion lining on the crimson areas.

The black goods and mixed traffic locomotive livery and its lining.

A Great Central Railway Manchester express of the early 20th Century illustrating the first carriage livery adopted for the new London Extension vehicles. Robinson Class '11B' 4-4-0 No. 1022 was built in February 1902.

Author's collection

Locomotives designated as 'goods' engines were painted black, specified as ivory black, the best grade of black oil paint. There was at first some fluidity over which types were which, and all the Class '8F' 'Immingham' 4-6-0s of 1906 were originally green (repainted black during 1908-9) and three of the six Class '1' 4-6-0s of 1912 were turned out in black, not changed to green until 1921-22.

Black locomotives had valances, splashers and boiler bands edged with a thin white line in conjunction with a thin vermilion one, the vermilion always being on the outer boundary. Cabs, tanks and tenders were panelled with a pair of white lines in a similar way to the green engines, but the outer white line was conjoined with a ½-inch vermilion band. Other features, such as bufferbeams and cab interiors, were treated the same as for green engines.

Mr Robinson introduced brass numberplates. At first these were rectangular with vermilion backgrounds, but by the appearance of the Class '9J' 0-6-0s in September 1901 had become elliptical. The vermilion background was retained briefly, but by October of that year was altered to black. Just inside the raised rim was a thin white line. Many ex-MS&LR and early GCR engines never received a plate at all, but retained gold transfer numbers.

Bufferbeams carried the usual "Nº [hook] number" in gold 4½ inch characters shaded in black, or in some cases light and dark blue. Most engines carried "GREAT [arms] CENTRAL" on tanks or tenders. This was in gold block letters 6 inches high, shaded to right and below in red, although there was a smaller version available for where there was limited space. In addition, most tender engines carried the coat of arms on the driving wheel splasher, if there was

room. The 'Jersey Lily' 4-4-2s had one on each splasher, but 4-6-0s had one centrally. The compound 4-4-2s had one on the leading splasher, with a "GCR" monogram on the second splasher. This monogram was also featured on Class '8C' and '8F' 4-6-0s.

After lining and lettering of both green and black engines, the smokebox, chimney, back of the firebox, platform (footplate), brake hangers and other black items which had all had one coat of black, were finished with black japan. The rest of the engine and tender received up to three coats of hard-drying finishing varnish.

At the time of the formation of the GCR, carriages were varnished teak. The carriage designs of Mr Parker had used conventional beading around the top quarter panels and the quarter lights, but had applied strips of half-round beading on the waist and bottom quarter panels, rather like the Great Northern Railway. However, it was decided that the new bogie carriages for the London Extension would depart from the traditional varnished finish and were to be painted. It is almost certain, therefore, that the new carriages were panelled in mahogany, which all painted carriages on other railways would have been. In addition, for these new carriages the upper quarter panels were to be omitted altogether and the windows and vertical panels taken right up to the cornice.

The company apparently modelled their new painted style on that of the London & North Western Railway. The bottom quarter panels were a dark brown similar to the L&NWR purple brown. Unfortunately, no specification has survived and so it is impossible to say whether a finishing coat of carmine lake was applied to make the colour identical to that of the other railway. One source does

The Manchester express passing Rickmansworth circa 1904. The carriages are in the Robinson brown and cream livery, but Class '8' 4-6-0 No. 1069, depicted here in green, was actually carrying the lined black livery when the photograph on which this painting was based was taken. *Author's collection*

Great Central Railway 50-foot clerestory Brake Third No. 1642 as built in 1903, carrying the then-current brown and cream livery. Note the shortened name 'Great Central', the lined ends to the headstocks and the beautiful etched glass in the lavatory window. *John Quick collection*

suggest in 1896 that the lower panels were to be painted 'lake', but from contemporary reports it seems it was an ordinary dark brown, possibly a purple brown. In fact, there is a report that called it a medium brown. For my purposes, I have used BS 381 412 Dark Brown (Pantone 1545).

Unlike L&NWR carriages, the GCR did not paint the upper beading brown. All above the waist was a light greenish grey, often referred to in sources as French grey, similar to the L&NWR flake white. Again, no specification has survived, but I would suggest that the greenish hue was probably brought about by layers of varnish over a pale lead grey slightly tinted with ultramarine blue. This was standard paint shop practice in an attempt to combat the yellowing effect of the varnish, and was again similar to the L&NWR's method. There is a British Standard French Grey (BS 381 630,

The brown and 'French grey' carriage livery 1897-1902.

Pantone 5635) which I believe has the right hue, although it is possibly a little too dark.

The whole upper two-thirds of the carriage was grey, the junction between the two colours being along the centre of the lower waist beading. The only dark brown feature above the waist was the cornice. Gold lining was applied to the centre of all the half-round beading, continued as a line between the two body colours even where there was no beading. Gold lining was also applied to the bottom of the sides and up each end. The grey upper panels were

lined only in gold on the return curve of their beading, which is hard to see in photographs. Carriage ends were dark brown, the half-round beading being lined with gold. Roofs were white when new.

Class marking in words appeared in the waist panels of the doors, and company lettering seems to have been "GREAT CENTRAL RAILWAY" in full, at least on the bogie stock. On this stock there were two numbers arranged symmetrically on each side, with the coat of arms placed below. Some special carriages had another placed centrally, so there were three coats of arms on each side.

Brown and 'cream' carriage livery 1902-1908.

Solebars were painted dark brown, edged with a broad band of black. Between the two colours was a yellow line. The ends of headstocks and the buffer casings were also lined in yellow. Bogies and other fitments below the solebar were black. Wood-centred Mansell wheels had these varnished, and wheel tyres were white when new. Although the new style was aimed specifically at the new carriages for the London services, a considerable number of the teak ex-MS&LR 6-wheel carriages were also painted in this new style.

From the start of Mr Robinson's tenure, there was a change of heart in the carriage and wagon department. First, the half-round beading on the bottom quarter panels and waists of carriage bodies was abandoned on new construction, and finally upper quarter panels reappeared. These, the vertical panels and lower body were all provided with conventional beading. Furthermore, it had been reported that it was difficult to keep the brown and grey carriages clean. Thus, from 1902 carriages were painted colours that were reminiscent of the GWR. Mr Robinson was of course trained at Swindon. The upper and waist panels were now painted a colour

The teak matchboard stock 1911.

specified as cream instead of grey. In the absence of further information, I have used the GWR cream (Carter 45, BS381 386 Champagne, Pantone 7508). The upper beading and the lower body below the waist were painted dark brown, specified simply as brown. The Parker-designed carriages, with their applied lower beading, were harder to accommodate to the new style and so the junction between the two colours was moved upwards to below the windows, the waist area on these carriages being brown. Whether the brown was the same as used previously is probable, but a moot point.

The new specification was to prepare the whole carriage with two coats of white lead, followed by filling and stopping as usual. Waist panels, upright panels and top quarter panels received a coat of cream colour, but the rest of the body was painted lead colour. The upper panels now received three coats of cream, and the lower panels and upper beading another coat of lead colour followed by two coats of brown. Lining was in gold following the edges of the beading. On bogie vehicles, what appears to have been a ⅛-inch yellow line follows the shape of the beading approximately half an inch outside the gold, joining together and running up the centre of the narrower beading strips. All below the body was black, including solebars, headstocks, footboards and buffer casings. The ends of headstocks and the buffer casings were lined, probably in yellow. Mansell wheel centres were varnished teak, and wheel tyres and roofs were white when new.

Class '9K' 4-4-2T No. 357 or 359 in full Robinson livery on a local train circa 1910, showing the teak (or painted and grained) carriage livery adopted in 1908.
Author's collection

Lettering in this period varied according to the type of coach. Characters were seriffed in gold 4½ inches high, shaded to right and below in black. Class marking was in words in the waist of each door. The arrangement of the other lettering was usually symmetrical, and where there was room (e.g. long waist panels on corridor sides or saloons) the name of the company was used in the form "GREAT CENTRAL", otherwise "G C R" was employed. On 6-wheel stock, this usually appeared to the left of a central door, with the number in the corresponding panel to the right. The coat of arms usually appeared twice on each side of bogie stock, but 6-wheel stock featured a script monogram "GCR" instead. Lavatory windows featured acid-etched renderings of the coat of arms.

From 1908, new stock was again built in teak and varnished. To provide a uniform carriage fleet, the existing carriages were now painted and grained to resemble teak as they went though shops. There is evidence to suggest that older ex-MS&LR local coaches were given the same treatment before 1908, and indeed it is possible that many of them were never painted at all. From 1910 new construction used vertical teak matchboarding on the bodies. Solebars in this later period were plain black, but roofs were still white.

Teak-panelled carriages were lined and lettered in gold, but the painted 'teak' carriages were lined and lettered in a stone colour paint, probably the usual painters' imitation gold colour. Carriage lettering was much simpler, being "GCR" and the number in 3-inch seriffed characters shaded in black, but class marking was now in large 9-inch numerals on each door.

The matchboarded teak carriages were unlined and employed seriffed brass characters about 5 inches high for the lettering and numbering in a strange, almost Art Nouveau, style. The large 'Barnum' saloons for excursion traffic featured "G.C.R" at each end with a central number, but the ordinary main line stock simply had "G.C.R" with the number below at each end. Class marking was in brass numerals on each door.

Non-passenger carriage stock was painted dark brown, lined and lettered in carriage style. Fitted fish vans until 1908 were also painted dark brown, lettered "G C" in yellow, but after that date were painted goods stock grey. On the adoption of the teak finish for passenger carriages, non-passenger stock was painted and grained to match.

Space rather limits the descriptions of the many types of wagon used by the Great Central Railway. Goods stock was painted a light medium grey, with black below the solebar. General stock was lettered "G C" as large as possible, usually about 18 inches high, in white seriffed characters. The position of tare and load lettering was extremely variable, but tare to the left and load to the right, often on the solebar only, seems to have been common. Numberplates were rectangular, with "GCR" over the number. There was also a white five-pointed star on solebars, used since MS&LR days. Some fitted vans were distinguished by large discs. There is evidence that some goods brake vans had red (vermilion) ends.

Cattle wagons, sleeper wagons and some other special vehicles carried "G.C.R" and the number on separate cast plates on the body. Worthy of note are the refrigerator vans, which had huge initials separated by an equally large five-pointed star, in white shaded with black, overwritten with "REFRIGERATOR" in black letters shaded in red.

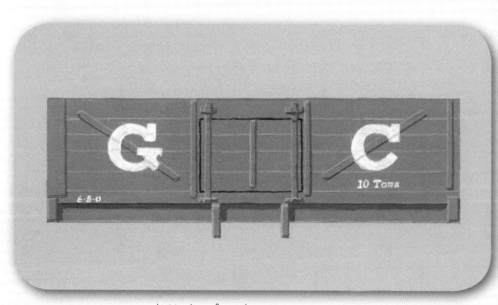

Lettering of goods open wagons.

1 'BRUNSWICK GREEN'
CARTER 15
PANTONE 350
BS 381 226
'MID BRUNSWICK GREEN'

2 'CRIMSON LAKE'
CARTER 27
PANTONE 1817
BS 381 449
'LIGHT PURPLE BROWN'

3 'VERMILION'
CARTER 36
PANTONE 485
BS 5252 04 E 55
OR BS 381 536
'POPPY RED'

✤ Great Eastern Railway ✤

This important railway was formed in 1862 from several companies, dominated by the Eastern Counties Railway, incorporated in 1836 for a line between London, Norwich and Yarmouth. The slow construction of its line from the Shoreditch terminus prompted other railways to fill the vacuum. By the mid-1840s four main groups had arisen: the Norfolk Railway, the East Anglian Railways, the Eastern Union Railway and the ECR.

Under the chairmanship of the infamous George Hudson, the ECR adopted an aggressive policy towards its neighbours. As the senior company with control of access into London, by 1850 the ECR had dominated all railways in the region except the EUR. When the EUR was leased in 1854, Parliament insisted that a Bill for amalgamation be presented by the end of 1861. This was done and the Great Eastern Railway came into being in 1862. There followed considerable expansion of lines in the London area and in East Anglia generally, and a new Liverpool Street station became fully operational in 1875. The company promoted growth in the agricultural economy of the region, diversified into shipping, hotels and bus services, provided better trains and expresses of the top rank.

Early locomotive superintendents followed each other in rapid succession: Mr Robert Sinclair (to 1866), Mr S.W. Johnson (1866-73), Mr W. Adams (1873-78), Mr Massey Bromley (1878-82) and Mr T.W. Wordsell (1882-85). A stable period followed with the Holdens: James (1885-1907) and son Stephen (1908-12). Mr A.J. Hill filled the post from 1912 to the Grouping, styled as 'Chief Mechanical Engineer' from 1915. The locomotives and rolling stock of the GER were built and cared for at Stratford Works, where the railway's large paint shop was situated.

The Great Eastern Railway became a constituent of the London & North Eastern Railway in 1923, and passed to the Eastern Region of British Railways in 1948.

Locomotives were originally green, lined out with black and vermilion. Mr Johnson is said to have darkened the green and painted buffer beams green also. Some engines were painted a yellow ochre colour (the exact shade has not been established) and were nicknamed 'canaries'. Under William Adams, locomotives were painted black, and this remained the standard until the 1880s. Engines fitted for passenger working were lined in red, but goods engines were unlined.

GER Class 'C32' 2-4-2T No. 1088, built in 1894, on a Southend train composed of close-coupled 4-wheel 'six-a-side' suburban carriages, near Brentwood.

Author's collection

It was in 1882 that the famous blue livery appeared [1]. At first it was applied to all engines, but from 1890 was restricted to passenger engines. Goods engines were then black, unlined, although some small shunting engines were lined in vermilion.

The blue livery consisted of a lead colour undercoat (also known in the Stratford paint shop as 'aluminium') covered with four coats of ultramarine blue and several coats of varnish. Experimentation with proper oil colours and varnish produces a dark but intense blue, which has led myself and others to disagree with Carter's colour patch (No. 24). In fact the colour is much closer to sample No. 25, which makes one wonder if an error in the text in the GER chapter of *Britain's Railway Liveries* has occurred, just as in the Great Western Railway section (see Volume One).

The blue areas were edged with a broad band of black, with a vermilion [2] line between the two colours. Wheel tyres and axle ends were black, lined with vermilion. Frames were black, including the upper parts above the footplate, except on the Class 'T19' rebuilt 4-4-0s, the 'Claud Hamilton' 4-4-0s and the Class 'S69' 4-6-0s, which had blue above the footplate.

Tender copings were unlined blue, but black on the large 3,450, 3,500 and 3,700 gallon tenders. Cab fronts were plain black. Cab interiors were buff, and buff was also applied between the frames. Cab roofs were white in official photographs, but were probably painted grey in service. Buffer beams and buffers were vermilion edged with black and lined in white, and the outer ends of the buffer casings were lined in the same way. Guard irons, where attached to buffer beams, were also vermilion.

The blue livery as first applied to existing engines had no lettering except the elliptical cast iron numberplates introduced by Mr Bromley in 1879, which had vermilion backgrounds. New

NIGEL J. L. DIGBY 1998

locomotives received a brass numberplate with a new lettering layout, and the initials "GER" in small 4½-inch letters. Lettering was in gold, shaded to left and below in white through yellow and red to brown, and shadowed in black. Bufferbeam lettering was in the form "Nº [hook] 567", in yellow serif characters of variable size, seven inches being the maximum, shaded to the left and below in brown. Only tank engines had the number on the rear bufferbeam.

From 1885 coupling rods were painted vermilion and company initials were enlarged to 6 inches, more widely-spaced. From circa 1893 all blue-painted tender engines carried the armorial device on the splasher. The 'Claud Hamilton' 4-4-0s are well-known as having painted cast-iron devices, but this was by no means universal, as several carried transfers at various times. The Class 'S69' 4-6-0s had no device at all.

The armorial device was a complicated one, consisting of eight shields bearing the arms of towns, cities and districts served by the GER circling the central arms of the City of London. Surrounding all was a garter carrying the words "GREAT EASTERN RAILWAY".

From 1915 locomotives were turned out of the paint shop in the grey undercoat colour. All parts that would have normally been black on blue engines remained black, including boiler bands, but there was no black edging to panels or lining of any kind. Coupling rods and numberplate backgrounds remained vermilion. Bufferbeams were at first lined as before, but later this was omitted and their lettering changed to white. Company initials were simplified to yellow shaded in vermilion. In 1921 large unshaded yellow serif numerals 18 inches high began replacing the company initials on tenders and tanksides, for train control purposes.

Carriage stock was built of teak on oak framing, and was turned out in a simple varnished finish with no lining. Solebars were painted and grained to resemble teak. Below the solebar was black, the centres of the Mansell wheels being varnished wood. It is believed that metalwork on the solebars was painted brown, including footboard brackets. Roofs were white or varying shades of grey; a common method was to paint the area below the rainstrips grey, and the rest white.

After a period of time in service (approximately fifteen to twenty years) a carriage's teak panelling would be painted teak colour. This colour was widely referred to as carriage brown or indeed 'Stratford brown', although its use was by no means unique to Stratford Works, as we have seen. Lining was now applied, but only to the quarter-lights and upright panels, being a ¼-inch yellow line (probably lemon chrome) on the top of the beading rather than on the return curve. Carriages built prior to 1886 had rectangular panels of half-

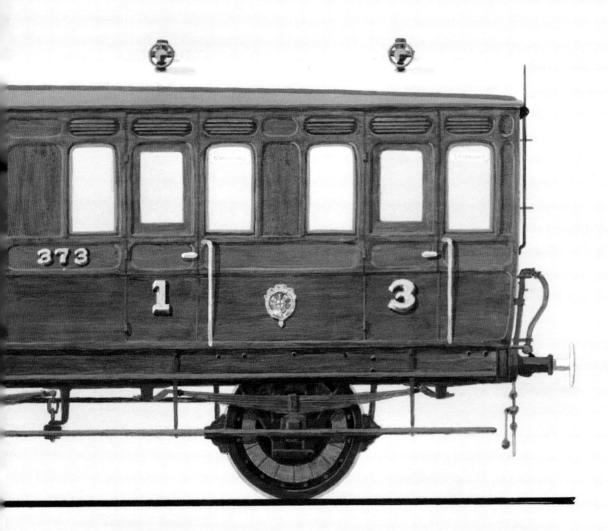

round beading applied at the waist, and unusually these were lined with a ½-inch black line only.

The standard lettering until 1902 was "GER" and the number, in the waist panels of main line stock, but in the top quarter panels of suburban and secondary stock, which was 4-wheeled. Class marking was "1ST", "2ND" or "3RD" in the waist panels of the doors. Lettering was sans-serif in gold, shaded in red and white, and shadowed in black. Main line First class carriages, and Composites containing First class, carried the armorial device on the lower body panels. Unlike the plain device of the locomotives, the carriage device featured gold filigree work surmounting the garter.

From 1902 the company initials on all stock were abbreviated to "GE", and large 12-inch class numerals on the bottom panels of doors superseded the class words. Otherwise, the lettering and device positions remained the same. The doors on some of the suburban stock built in the 1898 period featured roundels,

The Stratford Works carriage brown and yellow lining, as applied to a carriage built before 1885, with the extra black lining on the waist beading.

and the class markings transferred on them remained in 8-inch numerals.

From 1919, new stock and other stock as it came through shops was painted crimson lake [3]. Remains indicate that it was similar to the Midland Railway colour, but a little darker. The beading was lined out with ¼-inch lemon chrome lines, one each side of the beading strips, on the top of the beading rather than on the return curve, just as in the previous period. Remains indicate that there was actually more lining than some Stratford drawings would seem to imply. The lining emphasised the top quarter panels, waist panels and the quarter-lights (windows), but was not applied below the waist. Bogie stock had black underframes, but non-bogie vehicles had crimson solebars. The wood centres of Mansell wheels were also painted crimson. Carriage roofs were now entirely grey.

The lettering style changed to 4¼-inch seriffed characters, still in gold, shaded in red and white, shadowed in black, closely resembling the MR designs. Class numerals on mainline stock were reduced to 8 inches high over the gold, 9 inches overall. The carriage device was still used on the lower body panels of main line stock.

Coincident with the adoption of crimson lake for carriage stock, the GER instituted a new system for organising its intensive suburban services to Chingford, Enfield and Palace Gates, brought into operation in 1920. To assist the passenger, coloured stripes were painted along the top quarter panels of the 4-wheel 'six-a-side' suburban carriages to indicate class. First class was shown by a yellow strip, Second by blue, but Third class was simply the crimson body colour. Company initials and the number were still on these top panels, with class marking on the doors. The precise colours

The crimson carriage livery of 1919, taken from a surviving carriage body of 4-wheel 5-compartment Third No. 1262, built 1881 and withdrawn 1925 whilst still in GER livery.

used are not known, but the yellow was almost certainly chrome yellow, possibly lemon chrome, and the blue based on ultramarine, possibly lightened a little to be more visible. The public perceived these coloured stripes as being rather 'jazzy' in the spirit of the new popular music, and the nickname of 'Jazz trains' has persisted to the present day.

Goods stock was painted medium grey, including body and solebars. Ironwork below solebar level was black, together with buffer guides, drawbars and couplings. Lettering until 1902 was "GER" to the left and the number to the right of the body, in white 7-inch characters, with the same on the solebar in 3-inch characters.

From 1902 large initials appeared. For a very short time these were in a squared style, but from early in 1903 became the well-known "GE" initials, 24 inches high by 20 inches wide. The running

number was applied to the lower left plank of open wagons. Vans featured the initials on the third plank up, apparently with the number on the lower right. Cattle wagons had smaller 16-inch initials between the framing on the left-hand side, with the size of wagon on the right. Other special wagons had smaller initials to fit the available space.

Ventilated vans had the sides painted pale grey, with the standard lettering in black. Those fitted with the vacuum brake for foreign workings had the end panels of the body sides painted 'red', most probably red oxide rather than vermilion.

Brake vans usually had the initials widespread and the running number between, with the depot name on the second plank. There were, however, variations. According to the *Locomotive Magazine*, brake van headstocks (buffer beams) were painted vermilion.

GER wagon lettering before 1902, as applied to a standard unventilated van.

| **1** | 'ULTRAMARINE BLUE' CARTER 25 PANTONE 282 BS 381 105 'OXFORD BLUE' | **2** | 'VERMILION' CARTER 36 PANTONE 485 BS 5252 04 E 55 OR BS 381 536 'POPPY RED' | **3** | 'CRIMSON LAKE' CARTER 28 PANTONE 188 BS 381 540 'CRIMSON' |

Great Northern Railway

This railway, still part of the East Coast Main Line, was the result of an amalgamation between two rival schemes: the London & York and the Direct Northern, both initiated in 1844. The Great Northern Railway Act was passed in June 1846. The first section was opened in 1848, but the southern part of the main line from Peterborough to a temporary terminus in London opened in August 1850. The final part of the main line to Doncaster opened two years later, followed by King's Cross station in October 1852.

Trains ran to York over the North Eastern Railway north of Doncaster, and the GNR served Leeds, Bradford and the Yorkshire coalfields after traversing the West Riding & Grimsby Railway, a joint line with the Great Central Railway. The GNR participated in several other major joint lines: the Cheshire Lines, the Midland & Great Northern Joint Railway, the Great Northern and London & North Western Joint Railway, and the Great Northern & Great Eastern Joint Railway. Away from the main line, the major towns of Lincolnshire were served by the Lincolnshire Loop and the East Lincolnshire line to Grimsby. The branch to Nottingham and the Derbyshire lines left the main line at Grantham, and there were many smaller branches.

The GNR became a major constituent of the London & North Eastern Railway in 1923 and passed into the Eastern Region of British Railways in 1948.

Until about 1880, under the Locomotive Engineers Archibald Sturrock (1850-66) and Patrick Stirling (1866-95), the locomotive livery was a dark green, similar to that used by the Great Western, and frames were brown. At some point between 1876 and 1881, the main body colour was lightened to a colour likened to grass green [1], and the frames were changed to a deep red-brown often called claret, or simply 'lake' [2]. This famous scheme, detailed below, was carried on by Stirling's successors Henry Ivatt (1895-1911) and Herbert Nigel Gresley (1911-22) largely unchanged until the Grouping.

Details of locomotive livery are given by Doncaster drawing No. 44P of an Ivatt 0-6-0 in about 1900. Boiler and body panels above the footplate are light green, edged in black with a white line between the black and the green. Boiler bands are black, edged with white lines. Wheels are also light green with black tyres and axle ends. A black line edges the wheel boss, and each spoke has a black line down its centre. The tender has light green panels, edged with a dark green outer border. Between the two greens is a band

The 'Flying Scotsman' express near Hatfield behind celebrated Ivatt Class 'C1' 4-4-2 No. 990 *Henry Oakley* built in 1898, with a train of Howlden's finest clerestory stock, correctly shown with teak-colour side roofs and white clerestory roof.

Author's collection

of black fine-lined in white, forming a panel with incurved corners. Valances, engine and tender frames are in the dark red-brown, but here prosaically referred to as brown. This is edged in black with a vermilion line between the brown and the black. Guard irons are black. Buffer beams are vermilion [3], edged with black and a white line, but buffer casings are brown edged black at the outer end, lined in vermilion. The small part of the main frames above the footplate, the smokebox and the front cylinder cover are all black.

Although not on the drawing, it is known that main frames above the footplate of other engines were brown, lined in black and vermilion, but this seems reserved for the larger areas, as seen on the Atlantics for example. Outside cylinders were black, and on Stirling engines they were combined with the smokebox in one wrapper. A vestigial remnant of this practise seems to have survived on engines with both outside and inside cylinders, in which an area on the frames directly below the smokebox was painted black, forming a sort of saddle. This is evident on many photographs, particularly the Ivatt 'Singles' and the Atlantics. However, except for the Atlantics and other newer engines with exposed saddles above the cylinder castings, this practice had been abandoned by circa 1910.

Tanksides were treated in the same manner as tenders, having a dark green outer border and a panel of black and white lining. The lettering "G N R" was in 9 inch gold sans-serif characters, shaded to right and below in red and brown, with fine white lines adding definition. Numbers were applied to cabsides or bunkers of tank engines in a similar fashion. Single digit numbers were preceded by "Nº". Bufferbeam numbers were 7½-inch gold, shaded in brown and white. The usual arrangement, for example "Nº [hook] 282" was used. Many of the locomotives had brass beading to the splashers, and Stirling locomotives had polished brass safety valves. Smokebox door hinges and handles were polished steel.

From 1912, goods locomotives were painted dark grey with no lining. During the 1914-18 war, many passenger engines were also painted grey. Tenders and tanks had a single white line forming a panel, as usual with incurved corners. Lettering was in white, shadowed to right and below in black. From 1919 green and brown was reintroduced, but at the Grouping there were still many locomotives in grey.

RIGHT: Lining on upper locomotive frames as seen on Ivatt Class 'A4' and 'A5' 4-2-2 'Singles'.

NIGEL J. L. DIGBY 2000

The daily experience for the majority of GNR passengers would be of a train hauled by one of the many Ivatt 4-4-0s the railway possessed, such as Class 'D1' No. 1327. The dark green border to the tender and the vestigial black 'wrapper' on the frames below the smokebox are evident. *Author's collection*

Goods locomotive livery from 1912.

Until 1905, the carriage and wagon department was under the control of Mr E.F. Howlden, whose distinctive carriage panelling and very low elliptical roof profile (called the 'round roof' at Doncaster) became one of the trademarks of the GNR. As far as is known, carriages were always varnished teak. Solebars were painted 'teak colour', a light reddish brown. Wheels were of the teak-centred Mansell type with white tyres, the wood centres being varnished until discoloured, then painted teak colour. Ironwork below the

solebar was black. Roofs of main-line coaches were buff, but on the clerestory vehicles introduced in 1896 the portion of roof between cornice and clerestory was teak colour, as were the roofs of suburban stock.

Lining was in pale yellow (lemon chrome), fine-lined ultramarine blue on each side. It was applied on the half-round beading below the waist, and in vertical lines terminated at top and bottom with 'darts' on the upper beading. Lettering was in gold, seriffed characters

'GNR' monogram from carriage doors during the Howlden period.

about 3 inches high, shaded to left and below in blue, light blue and white, shadowed in black. Most carriages had "G N R" and the number on each side. Class marking was in smaller words on the waist panel of the doors, although suburban carriages had large seriffed 9-inch class numerals instead.

Some of the best bogie express stock carried the elaborate 'coat of arms', two per side, which (as it was not registered with the College of Heralds) should really be termed a 'device'. Ordinary carriages had a gold "GNR" monogram 6 inches high on all the lower door panels. For this monogram, the "G" and the "R" were elaborate letters in light and dark shades of gold to give three-dimensional form, but the "N" consisted of a bolder letter in blue edged with gold. This made it stand out, and on most contemporary black and white photographs it appears to be white, an illusion caused by the orthochromatic emulsion's sensitivity to blue. The company seemed to feel that the emphasis on the 'Northern' was important, the same appearing on the goods wagons.

Mr H.N. Gresley introduced new designs of bogie carriage, incorporating high elliptical roofs. The varnished teak remained, but the old buff roofs were superseded by white, and larger lettering was introduced, about 4½ inches high over the gold. Many new carriages were lettered "GREAT NORTHERN." in full (with full stop), also with "DINING SALOON." or other lettering where appropriate. Where initials were used, they were now "G.N.R." with prominent full stops. Full stops also appeared after the numbers. Class marking was now in numerals and abbreviations "1$\underline{\text{ST}}$" or "3$\underline{\text{RD}}$" on the door waist panels, with dashes under the abbreviations. Older stock generally retained its former styling, but the monograms were no longer used.

Non passenger-carrying vehicles such as horseboxes and carriage trucks were painted teak colour, described (typically) as 'light umber brown'. The lettering, usually "G.N.R." and the number, was in yellow sans-serif characters, but shaded in blue and white, as for the passenger stock.

Gresley carriage lettering.

Ordinary goods wagons were painted oxide brown [4], sometimes called 'chocolate'. This was a warm reddish brown. The first lettering was "G NORTHERN R" in white sans-serif characters, the initials being about 6 inches and the rest of the middle word being 5 inches. It was placed on the left; on wagons with low sides or restricted room it was arranged in one line, but on larger areas it was arranged vertically, with the "G" and the "R" placed centrally above and below the "NORTHERN". The number was painted in a corresponding position on the right. To the lower left, usually on the bottom rail, was the load restriction in smaller, thinner characters, for example "LOAD 9 TONS". On the solebar was a rectangular plate carrying "G.N.R." over the number, with white characters and border.

From 1898 the large letters "G N" were introduced, although the former lettering survived on older wagons for several years. The letters were as large as possible on the wagon, up to a maximum of 2 feet 6 inches. A number of wagons received a small "G.N.R." in white around the turn of the century, and some which were fitted and intended for use in passenger trains seem to have the same in gold or yellow lettering shaded in blue. With the large initials, the number was placed on the right of the lower rail opposite the load, or was not painted on the body at all. Special uses were usually painted centrally, for example "FISH TRUCK", "LOCO" or "FRUIT VAN".

Refrigerator vans were white, some with brown oxide solebars, and black lettering. Gunpowder vans were also white, but with red lettering. Brake vans in the older period had the number central at the top, "G NORTHERN R" below and "GOODS BREAK" below that, but this lettering was abandoned when the large lettering was adopted, the number then usually being painted centrally between the two initials.

Wagon sheets were marked with "G N R" and the number on each side, and had a diagonal cross formed of one white line from corner to corner, crossed by one blue line to the other corners.

Original wagon lettering until circa 1898.

1 'LIGHT GREEN'
CARTER 10
PANTONE 349 (APPROX)
BS 381 221
'BRILLIANT GREEN'

2 'CLARET'
CARTER 30
PANTONE 4695
BS 381 490
'BEECH BROWN'

3 'VERMILION'
CARTER 36
PANTONE 485
BS 5252 04 E 55
OR BS 381 536
'POPPY RED'

4 'BROWN OXIDE'
CARTER 29
PANTONE 483
BS 381 448
'DEEP INDIAN RED'

Great North of Scotland Railway

In the north-east of Scotland a small railway with its headquarters in the granite city of Aberdeen maintained a proud service with excellent carriages and a locomotive fleet consisting mainly of small but graceful 4-4-0s. But it had not always been thus. For the first thirty years of its existence the 'Great North' earned itself a very poor reputation. The first section was opened in 1854 and the main line was completed in 1856. Expansion by a series of branches followed. At Keith, Inverness traffic was handed over to the Highland Railway, whose line over the mountains to Perth had been a direct result of the Great North's reluctance to extend its main line, its poor treatment of passengers and its roundabout route.

Improvements did come, and eventually there were lines built beyond Keith, but its services were poor and expensive. However, a turnabout in the railway's fortunes was not far off. A new General Manager appeared on the scene, Mr W. Moffatt, and henceforth the Great North gradually reformed. A new coast line to Elgin was opened in 1886 and express trains, a novelty for the railway, were introduced with new stock. On the appointment of William Pickersgill as Locomotive, Carriage & Wagon Superintendent in 1894, the Great North's star was definitely in the ascendent. The *Railway Magazine* in the late 1890s devoted many pages in praise of it and coined the phrase 'Little and Good' to describe it, a nickname that has stuck ever since.

The workshops of the company were at first established at Kittybrewster near Aberdeen, but because of the cramped nature of the site, a new works was established by 1902 at Inverurie, some fifteen miles outside the city.

The Great North became a constituent of the London & North Eastern Railway in 1923, and passed to the Scottish Region of British Railways in 1948.

As far as is known, in the earlier periods Great North of Scotland Railway locomotives were painted green, with black and white lining. The shade of green, the style of lining and other details changed under the various Locomotive Superintendents: William Cowan (1857-83), James Manson (1883-90) and James Johnson (1890-94). Bringing the railway into more modern times, and probably the most important period for the modeller, were William Pickersgill (1894-1914) and Thomas Heywood (1914-22), and it is on their practices that I will concentrate.

Locomotives under Mr Pickersgill were a light chrome green, apparently similar to that of the North Eastern Railway [1]. Lining was in black and vermilion [2]. Most body panels were edged with black and fine-lined vermilion. Tenders, tanks and cabsides had a further border of a dark green. The application of this border on cabs varied between classes. Normally, when driving wheel splashers were separated from cabs by beading (for example the Class 'T' 4-4-0s), the border was confined to the cab itself, but if splashers and cabs were combined (as on the Class 'V' 4-4-0s), these were all bordered as one. Within this border was a single vermilion line with incurved corners. Boiler bands were black, fine-lined vermilion, and valances and steps were edged with black and a vermilion fine-line. Wheels were green with black tyres, lined vermilion. Axle ends were usually black, and wheel bosses could also be edged with black and vermilion.

Bufferbeams were vermilion, being edged with black and a white fine-line, the buffers dividing the lining into panels. Numbers were displayed on front bufferbeams, for example "Nº [hook] 23", in gold

A Valentine 'Artotype' postcard showing one of many occasions that the Great North of Scotland Railway conveyed the Royal Family to Ballater, the nearest station to Balmoral. The first three vehicles are GNSR stock.   *Author's collection.*

sans-serif characters shaded with blue-grey and white. The same was also placed in the middle of the rear of tenders and bunkers, rather than on the rear bufferbeams.

Numberplates were brass, with sunken letters filled with black wax, having "GREAT NORTH OF" above and "SCOTLAND RAILWAY" below the central number, which was preceded by "Nº". The plates were outlined on the body panels in black and vermilion.

Lettering on tenders and tanksides was "G . N . S . R ." in gold sans-serif characters, shaded in red to the right and below, with white highlights. The full stops were placed equidistantly between each letter. Locomotives built by the outside contractor Neilson, Reid & Co. of Glasgow (later part of the North British Locomotive Company) were lettered without full stops and appeared in a darker green, replaced by the standard livery during their first repaint at Inverurie.

A Valentine's Series postcard of a GNSR 4-4-0. These cards were not known for their colour accuracy but do show the lining and lettering arrangements.

Author's collection

NIGEL J.L. DIGBY 2003

From 1916, under Mr Heywood, black was adopted for all locomotives. Lining was restricted to a vermilion line near panel edges, with a yellow line a short distance within. Valances reversed this practice, being edged with yellow. Boiler bands were edged with vermilion and had a yellow line up the centre. The last batch of 4-4-0s built in 1920 were turned out in black and, unusually, were named. Lettering on the black livery remained the same, but numberplates on new engines and some others were changed. They now had raised brass characters and border, possibly on a vermilion background. The central number was larger than formerly, seriffed, and no longer preceded by "Nº". The armorial device, a shield featuring the arms of Aberdeen and the Royal Scottish lion surrounded by a garter, also made its only appearance during this period. It featured on the splashers of the 4-4-0s and on the bunkers of tank engines.

Unfortunately the preserved engine No. 49 *Gordon Highlander* has been turned out in a green livery (which it would not have had) but lined out in the black style; another faux pas by the early preservationists.

Until 1883, the standard specification for carriages was varnished teak. The specification was typical of the way teak carriages were treated on all railways. First the wood was prepared with one coat of gold size, followed by eight coats of body varnish (flatted each time after the third coat), and one coat of best finishing varnish. Roofs were painted white lead. The solebars were painted 'teak colour' and varnished. Ironwork on the body and solebar, such as footboard brackets, was to be painted green and 'bronzed' (see glossary, this volume). Other ironwork on the underframe, including springs, buffer casings and brake gear was to be painted black and japanned. Buffer heads and shafts were to be finished bright metal. Lettering during this period was abbreviated to "G.N.S." and the number, with class marking in words, the initial letter being taller.

A panel of Mr Heywood's black locomotive livery.

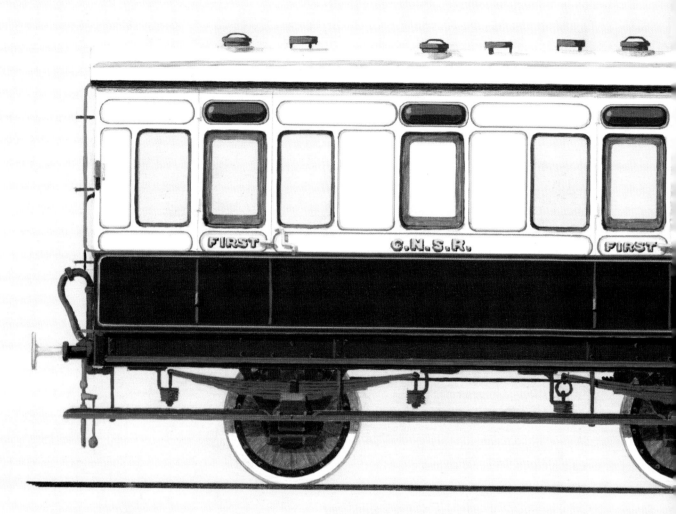

From 1883, the specification was changed to the cheaper option of mahogany body panels with a painted finish. From a specification of December 1895, the colour used was crimson, obtained in the usual way by using a brown undercoat, glazed with three coats of crimson lake and finished with five coats of varnish. Fascias were painted black, lined around the edges in gold leaf, fine-lined with vermilion. Headstocks, solebars and footboards were painted black, then japanned and varnished. Droplights were varnished wood and roofs were lead white. Mansell wheels were varnished, with black ironwork and white tyres.

The lettering style was now "G.N.S.R." and the class words had letters all the same size. The prefix "Nº" was introduced before the number. Lettering was sans-serif in gold, shaded in red, highlighted in white and shadowed in black. Altogether, Great North carriages assumed a very Midland Railway aspect, particularly on the arrival of Mr Johnson, who had trained under his father Samuel Johnson of the Midland. He adopted conventional bottom, waist and upper panels and fascias with curved corners throughout, rather than the square Great Northern-type styling on the bottom quarter panels preferred formerly.

In December 1895, Mr Pickersgill suggested that an attractive new livery be applied, combining white with a darker crimson,

which he called purple lake [3]. This colour was very reminiscent of the London & North Western and Caledonian carriage colour. The top colour, possibly carmine rather than alizarin crimson, was transparent and relied heavily on the undercoat brown for the final colour. In order to impart the so-called purple sheen to the finished livery, this brown was very likely to be similar to the dark purple brown of the L&NWR, which was a mix of 10½ lb black and 9 lb of Indian red.

From 1896 most carriages were henceforth turned out in purple lake, with white applied to everything above the waist, including the beading or fascias. Older vehicles were given an all-over purple lake finish. The white was specified as Kremnitz white (lead white), which, thanks to the many coats of varnish, would have appeared to have a slight ivory appearance. The only exceptions to the white above the waist were the top quarter panels of doors carrying ventilators, and the ventilators themselves, which remained purple lake, and the cornice, which was black. Lining was still ¼-inch gold, fine-lined with ⅛-inch vermilion. The junction of the two body colours was along the lower waist beading and was marked by a ⅛-inch line of vermilion, which merged with the vermilion fine-lining of the panels. By 1914, the gold had been replaced by yellow.

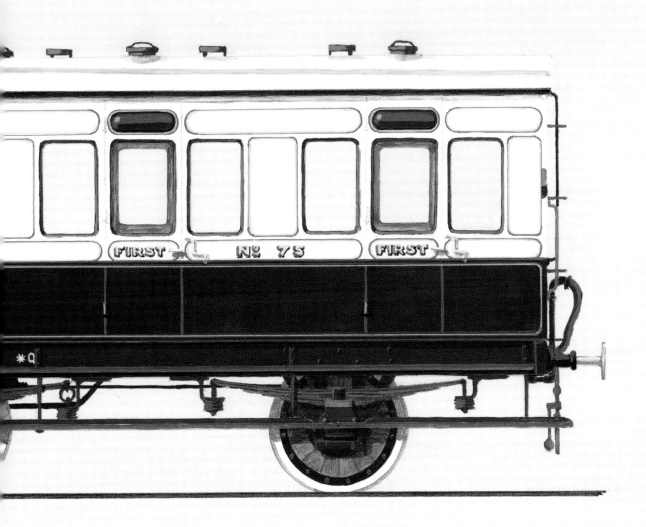

Most other details remained unchanged from the earlier syle. Lettering was in gold, shaded as before. Class words on the door waist panels were about 3 inches high. Company lettering was placed on each side of the central doors of 6-wheel vehicles, or as near to equidistantly on bogie stock as possible, about one third of the carriage length apart, being "G.N.S.R." on the left and "Nº [number]" on the right, in about 4-inch sans-serif characters.

Other coaching vehicles, horseboxes and so on, were originally unlined purple lake, and lettered in yellow with shading as described above. It is understood that by 1914 a paint called Colcother brown was used on this stock and other old vehicles on the duplicate

list. This was a dark red-brown pigment also known as purple brown, derived from calcining yellow ochre. Lettering was in plain unshaded yellow.

Goods stock was originally described as dark red, possibly brown oxide, but from circa 1896 a dark grey was adopted for general stock. It is not thought that company initials were used in the earlier period other than the numberplates. Numberplates were rectangular, with raised white characters on a black background, carrying "GREAT NORTH" above, and "OF SCOTLAND RAILWAY" below the number. When grey was introduced, it was lettered in large (approximately 16-inch) white characters "GNS", the "N" being central, even over the joints of van doors. The letters were usually placed in the middle of open wagon sides, or slightly above the middle of van sides, but loco coal wagons had the initials along the lower planks, with "LOCO COAL" above. Later numberplates were slightly changed from formerly, having "G.N.S.R." above the number and the load below, for example "LOAD 10 TONS".

Brake vans and service stock remained in dark red, and brake vans reportedly had vermilion ends.

Wagon sheets are recorded in 1896 to have carried the lettering "G.N.S.R." with no other recorded distinguishing marks. Apparently, the lettering was later altered to "G.N.S.", similar to that on the wagons, painted with the number in large characters on all four sides of the sheet with a very small "G.N.S." below.

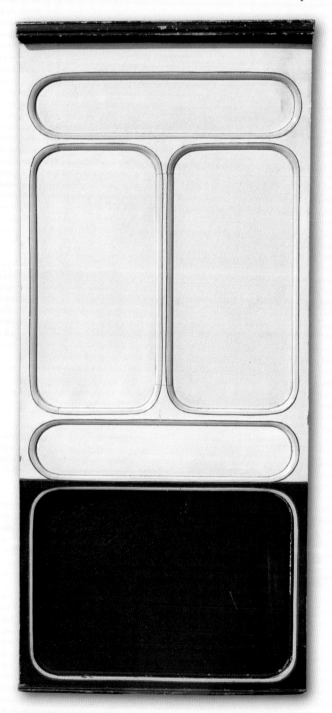

1 'LIGHT GREEN'
CARTER 3
PANTONE 363
RAL 6017 'MAY GREEN'

2 'VERMILION'
CARTER 36
PANTONE 485
BS 5252 04 E 55
OR BS 381 536
'POPPY RED'

3 'CARRIAGE PURPLE LAKE'
CARTER 43
PANTONE 4975
BS 381 541 'MAROON'

LEFT: The quarter-scale sample panel prepared by painters at Inverurie, showing the purple lake and white livery. The colours are seen under the effects of aged varnish.
Courtesy Keith Fenwick and GNRS Association

❧ Hull & Barnsley Railway ❧

The Hull, Barnsley & West Riding Junction Railway & Dock Company was incorporated in 1880 in an attempt to break the monopoly of the North Eastern Railway and to provide a new outlet for the coal export traffic from the south Yorkshire coalfield to the port of Hull. The Alexandra Dock in Hull was built by the railway, which with its later extension covered 53½ acres. The line was opened in 1885 and from 1905 the name was officially simplified to Hull & Barnsley Railway, but it had probably been known by that title for many years. The H&BR connected with many of the pits in the Barnsley coal seam, but at first passenger trains ran only from Hull (Cannon Street) to Cudworth (Midland Railway) or Knottingley (Lancashire & Yorkshire). In 1905 running powers were granted over the MR from Cudworth into Sheffield, and services began between there and Hull. Further pits were served by a 1902 branch to Wath. Finally, access to more southern areas was gained by a joint line with the Great Central Railway opened in 1916, the final portion of which was also joint with the MR.

This small but fascinating railway, with a total route of about 120 miles including joint lines, was amalgamated with the NER in 1922. It therefore became a part of the London & North Eastern Railway in 1923 and passed into the North Eastern Region of British Railways in 1948. Ten years later this was merged with the Eastern Region.

For the opening of the line, the company ordered locomotives from Beyer, Peacock & Co. and rolling stock from several of the leading contractors. Designs were prepared by Mr William Kirtley of the London, Chatham & Dover Railway in a consultative capacity. They all followed a very typical LC&DR outline and the similarity also extended to the liveries. As delivered, locomotives were black, lined with wide grey bands edged on each side with vermilion. They were provided with elliptical brass number plates bearing the long title of the railway in very small characters: "HULL BARNSLEY & WEST RIDING" over and "JUNCTION RAILWAY & DOCK Cº" under the large seriffed numerals. Lettering as delivered was "HB&WRJR" in a gold script monogram, shaded in red like the LC&DR monograms were, but this style did not last long.

From May 1885 the position of locomotive superintendent was filled by Matthew Stirling, son of the famous Patrick Stirling of the Great Northern Railway, who followed the domeless Stirling tradition when designing his own engines and rebuilding the original stock. Mr Stirling altered the manner of painting engines into a scheme that remained unchanged throughout the railway's existence. The body colour was known as 'invisible green', applied to boiler and firebox clothing, splashers, wheels, tanks and tenders. All the usual black areas of locomotives, such as main frames, platform (footplate), smokebox and chimney, back of firebox, wheel tyres, brake gear and so on were painted drop black and japanned.

Unlike other reported examples of so-called invisible green, which were invariably simply black, on the H&BR it was a real

Matthew Stirling Class 'J' 4-4-0 No. 38, built by Kitson & Co. in 1910, showing the rather exotic lining, and the device present on only this class of five locomotives.

Author's collection

colour and the precise constituents are known. It was specified as drop black mixed with an equal amount of Brunswick green. The resulting colour was very dark, and could easily be mistaken for black, except under bright sunlight or in comparison to true black. It falls between Pantone Black 3 and Pantone 5605. The nearest conventional paint colour is BS 4800 14 C 40 'Conifer'. This would probably be suitable for a model, but would need more black added to it to paint something full-size.

Tenders and tanksides were lined with very wide bands of ultramarine blue, fine-lined with vermilion. The panels of lining

Class 'A' 0-8-0 No. 117 built by the Yorkshire Engine Co. in 1907. The cab is lined in a panel on this first batch of ten, but the batch of five delivered later in the year had the lining carried over the cab roof.   *Author's collection*

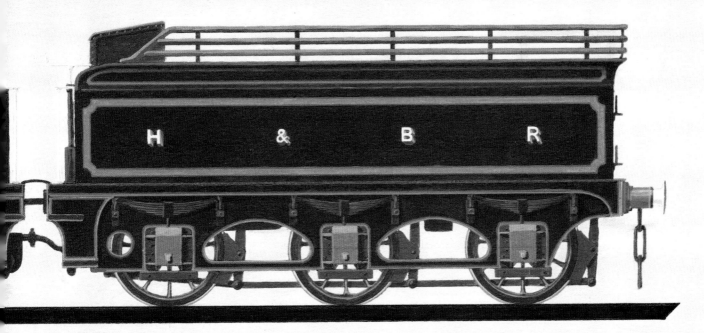

had incurved corners. Ordinary cabs were lined with blue bands following the shape of the side sheets, but the Stirling wrap-over cabs were lined in a continuous panel over the roof and down to the other side. Boiler bands were also painted ultramarine blue, edged with vermilion.

Above the platform, splashers, sandboxes and other small panels were edged with a thin line of blue, again fine-lined with vermilion. Below the platform, although there are some photographs indicating the use of blue, there is a strong case for suggesting that it was more common to line out with vermilion only, this being on valances, footsteps, wheel centres and wheel tyres. Apparently a yellow line could also be featured in conjunction with the vermilion. Buffer beams were vermilion bordered with black edged in yellow, and buffer casings were also lined with black edged in yellow at base and tip. Cab interiors were painted Indian red and edged with black and fine-lined vermilion, with a yellow line inside that.

Lettering was a widely-spaced "H & B R" in 6-inch characters on tender and tank sides. On new engines and later rebuilds, numbers were gilt transfers. All were in gold with red and white shading. The original engines built by Beyer Peacock retained their distinctive curved brass builder's plates over the splashers, and the elliptical numberplates tended to survive rebuilding, unless the cab was replaced at the same time.

In the *Railway Year Book*, carriage colour is given as dark green. However, the original specification for carriage livery was varnished teak, just as on the LC&DR. The carriages were 4-wheel with

Locomotive transfer numbering and typical lining of Stirling 'wrapover' cabs.

panelling identical to that of the LC&DR carriages. Solebars and wheel centres were painted teak colour. Below the solebar was black. Wheel tyres and roofs were white.

Carriage lettering as delivered was in gold characters 3 inches high, shaded in crimson and shadowed in black, which is believed to have been the LC&DR style (see Volume Four). Class marking in words appeared on each door, or "GUARD" where appropriate. Carriages were in four groups, all with differing lettering arrangements. The Composites and Thirds had no initials, but two numbers arranged symmetrically in the waist. The armorial device (see below) was placed below each number on the Composites, but Thirds had the script monogram "HB&WRJR", as used on the locomotives. The Brake Thirds had one number placed centrally, with the script monogram below it. Only on the Luggage Brakes did the initials feature; they were placed in the waist on the left of the central ducket in the form "H B & W R J R", omitting the dock reference. The vehicle number was placed on the waist of the ducket.

By 1897, and probably several years earlier, there had been some changes. Bodies were now lined in thin yellow lines on each side of the beading strips. Lettering was still in gold, but now shaded in blue. As the locomotives and the wagons adopted the initials "H&BR" around this time, it seems likely that the carriages did, too. Unfortunately, there is no photographic evidence from this period.

The rather florid armorial device was used on carriages, but only ever featured on one class of locomotives, the Class 'J' 4-4-0s. The design juxtaposes the arms of Kingston-upon-Hull and Barnsley,

with the winged wheel representing the railway and two entwined dolphins representing the docks. This was enclosed in a quatrefoil and encircled by a garter bearing the words "HULL AND BARNSLEY RAILWAY COMPANY". In the earlier period, the full title was used.

The original 4-wheel stock was used for all services into the early years of the 20th century. It had been planned to purchase 6-wheel carriages in 1899, but their cost had prevented this. However, it was considered desirable to acquire bogie vehicles for the through Sheffield services, which began in 1905. Twelve coaches were ordered from R.Y. Pickering & Co., delivered in 1907, and thirteen from Birmingham Railway Carriage & Wagon Co., delivered in 1909. In the interim, Midland Railway carriages were used for the Sheffield trains.

The bogie coaches were all in varnished teak, with solebars and wheel centres painted in teak colour. Buffer casings were black. Lining was in gold on each side of the beading and panels. Lettering was in gold, shaded in blue to right and below. Class marking was in words, as before, and coaches now had company initials "H & B R" in 6-inch lettering arranged symmetrically at each end, and all classes had a central number of the same size. The Birmingham RC&W carriages featured the device below the central number.

Non-passenger vehicles (horseboxes and carriage trucks) were painted teak colour and varnished. Ironwork was painted black. Lettering was originally in gold with crimson and black shading, just as for the passenger vehicles. The initials "H B & W R J R" were spaced along the upper body, with the number below, preceded by

"Nº". By 1897, lettering had become "H&BR" in yellow, shaded in black.

The *Railway Year Book* notes that Hull & Barnsley Railway wagons were dark blue. However, wagon specifications from the first state clearly that two coats of dark lead colour were used, finished with a final coat of dark lead mixed with varnish (an enamel). From photographs the H&BR dark lead grey was apparently a darkish grey, but not as dark as the shade used on the GWR. Below the solebar was black, and the body metalwork was treated with black japan by the makers, but it is thought that in service it may have been painted the body colour. Refrigerator vans were painted white.

Class 'F1' 0-6-2T No. 101 was one of five built by Kitson & Co. for the Lancashire, Derbyshire & East Coast Railway, but were delivered to the H&BR in 1901.

Author's collection

NIGEL J. L. DIGBY 1995

Wagons originally featured the company initials in full. A photograph of an original cattle wagon shows the body lettered on each side of the central door "H B & W R [door] J R & D Cᵒ" in about 6-inch characters. The number was placed on the lower right in the same size numerals. The rectangular numberplate had incurved corners and was lettered in a similar fashion, with "HB&WR" over the central number, and "JᶜRʸ&DᴷCᵒ" below.

By 1897, and probably earlier, body lettering was simplified to "H & B R" in large characters up to 18 inches high, although the numberplates retained the official title. Numbers were still on the lower right. Later, probably from 1905, the plate lettering changed to simply "H&BR" over the number.

It seems that towards 1914 the company took the opportunity for advertising on a number of wagons, "CONTINENTAL ROUTE VIA HULL" appearing on open wagons and vans, the arrangements varying considerably. At the time of this change, numbers seem now to have been placed on the right, and the load and tare notes also swapped positions.

Wagon sheets are noted in 1896 as carrying the letters "H & B R" and marked by a diagonal cross made up of one white stripe crossed by one red.

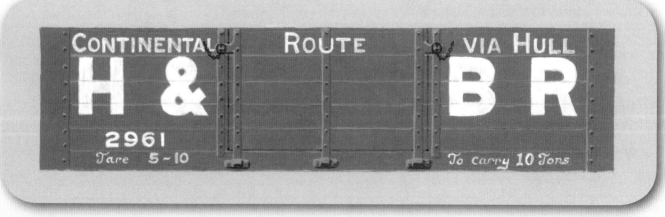

Later wagon lettering with advertisement.

Lancashire, Derbyshire & East Coast Railway

This grandiose scheme for linking the coalfields of north Derbyshire and Nottinghamshire with the west and east coasts of England obtained its Act in 1891. Difficulties in raising the required capital encouraged the railway to form an alliance with the Great Eastern Railway, which was keen to participate in the projected coal traffic. The GER urged the construction of the central portion from Chesterfield to Lincoln (Pyewipe Junction) first, with a branch from Langwith Junction to Beighton near Sheffield to serve the north Derbyshire town of Clowne and the collieries nearby. Construction began in 1892. Further difficulties in 1894 caused the LD&ECR Directors to approach the GER for help again. The GER's terms were abandonment of the proposed western section to Warrington, transfer of the proposed eastern section to the Lincolnshire coast to a separate company, and running powers over the entire railway. These terms were reluctantly accepted and any attempts to build the eastern section were finally abandoned in 1902.

The official opening in March 1897 was rather subdued; the LD&ECR had been reduced considerably from a grand 'East to West' main line to a local line handing most of its traffic over at Lincoln. However, coal was the reason for the railway and in this regard it fulfilled its promise admirably, nevertheless passenger traffic was limited. The Board of Directors had hopes of promoting the tourist aspects of the area, adopting the title of 'The Dukeries Route'. This met with some success, but local traffic was light despite the opening of the Sheffield District Railway in 1900, giving access to Sheffield (Midland) station. The railway's workshops were near Tuxford, at the point where the line crossed over the Great Northern Railway main line, known as Dukeries Junction, but Chesterfield Market Place station was the headquarters of the line.

After a working life of only ten years, the LD&ECR was absorbed by the Great Central Railway in 1907. It bequeathed a very healthy mineral traffic to its successor, a fitting tribute to its promoters. However, the short duration of the company means that modern researchers have little to go on, and those few references that do survive are frequently contradictory. It has not helped, for example, that the first paragraph of the LD&ECR section in E.F. Carter's *Britain's Railway Liveries* has been transposed from its true position in the Manchester, Sheffield & Lincolnshire section. Fortunately, I have been able to examine several very clear photographs from the Ian Allan library, which have helped to resolve many questions.

The LD&ECR locomotive department saw a rapid succession of Superintendents, but none of these, except perhaps the last one, Mr R.A. Thom, had any effect on the locomotives, which were all ordered from Kitson & Co. of Leeds. The four classes were all tank engines: eighteen Class 'A' 0-6-2Ts, four Class 'B' 0-6-0Ts, six Class

Class 'C' 0-4-4T No. 18 with a LD&ECR train circa 1900. The unusual characters of the 'Nº' are shown to advantage.

Author's collection

'C' 0-4-4Ts, and finally nine Class 'D' 0-6-4Ts, three of which were actually delivered after the GCR takeover.

Locomotive livery was black. Bufferbeams were vermilion [1], edged in black, with a fine white line between the black and the vermilion. Buffer casings were black. The engine number appeared on the bufferbeam in the usual way, "N⁰ [hook]18" for example, in large gold seriffed characters, shaded to right and below in blue and white. Beneath the "⁰" was a dash underscored by two square full stops. On the tanksides, the letters "L D & E C R" were spaced out in 6-inch gold characters shaded to right and below in blue and white. Cab interiors were a light buff or 'stone' colour. Coupling rods were painted vermilion, except on the Class 'C' 0-4-4Ts. Motion, motion brackets and inner faces of the frames were reportedly painted a rather unusual light blue.

The eighteen Class 'A' 0-6-2Ts (with the exceptions noted below) remained in unlined black, but the other locomotives were given an unusual and distinctive lining. References to this lining are contradictory, but photographs in the Ian Allan Bucknall Collection are irrefutable. The main panels of the body above the footplate; tanks, bunkers, cabs, splashers and sandboxcs, were lined in bands of light blue with ordinary curved corners, fine-lined on each edge with yellow. Following these bands at a distance of about 1½ inches on each side were fine lines of vermilion. Tanks, bunkers, cabs, valancing and steps were edged with a narrow band, which appears to have been blue with a yellow fine-line. On the valancing and steps this was again followed by a fine vermilion line at a short distance inside. Boiler bands were edged with a very narrow light line, which was probably the blue/yellow composite again. Vermilion fine-lining appeared on the boiler to each side. No lining appears to have been applied on wheels or frames. The black buffer casings were lined in blue and vermilion just behind their outer lip.

The first eight Class 'A' 0-6-2Ts of 1895 were actually delivered in the fully-lined livery, but later after repainting at Tuxford remained unlined. They also differed in that they did not originally have numberplates. The number was applied to the bunker in transfers and surrounded by a rectangle of gold or yellow paint in imitation of a plate, outlined by a fine vermilion line. All subsequent engines were given brass numberplates of the same shape as the painted imitation, being rectangular with rounded corners and subtly curved ends, bearing the engine number in polished brass serif

NIGEL J.L. DIGBY 2002

numerals on a vermilion background. They too were outlined in vermilion. Strangely, when the earliest Class 'A' engines were later given numberplates, they were actually more rectangular, without the slightly curved ends.

The most powerful engine on the line, Class 'A' 0-6-2T No. 26, was required to work the Royal Train when it regularly appeared conveying King Edward VII during the Doncaster Races. For the purpose, it was lined out in the style of the 'passenger' engines in 1903 and remained like this subsequently.

When taken over by the Great Central, it appears that all ex-LD&ECR locomotives were painted in the GCR goods livery of black lined in white and vermilion (see p. 111), and carried "GREAT [arms] CENTRAL" on the tanks. All were renumbered and fitted with Robinson elliptical numberplates. However, there is a photograph of the last LD&ECR engine to be delivered, the final Class 'D' 0-6-4T, carrying Great Central lettering and its new number 1147 while plainly lined out in the former style.

Carriages, apart from ten 4-wheelers secondhand from the GER, were built by Brown, Marshalls & Co. and Ashbury & Co. between 1896 and 1898. They were all 6-wheel and very similar

A panel of standard LD&ECR locomotive lining.

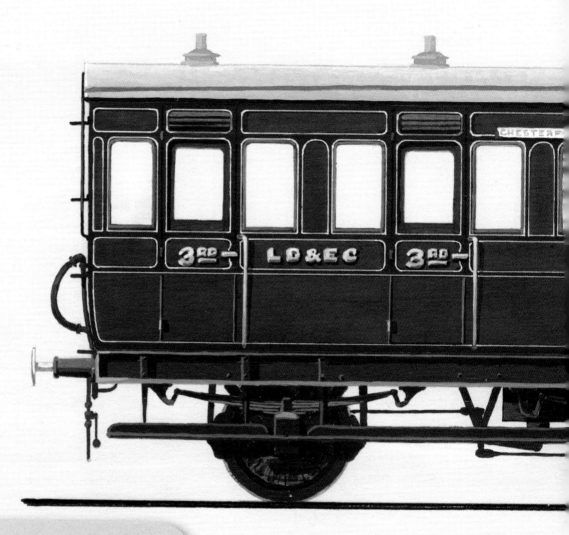

to contemporary GER carriages. Carriage livery was apparently a close copy of that of the Midland. The main colour was described as 'bright lake' or 'red brown', being a crimson lake allegedly a little lighter than the Midland colour [2]. Beading was painted black, edged with gold lining, and a fine vermilion line between the gold and the black. The underframes of these carriages were steel, and were painted black. Roofs were light grey.

Carriage lettering and numbering remained standard throughout the life of the company. The initials "L D & E C" were applied in the waist panels to the left-hand side of the vehicle, usually between the first and second compartments, with the number in

LEFT: A scrap view of the later carriage livery and lettering.

RIGHT: Class 'D' 0-6-4T No. 33 built by Kitson & Co. in 1904. The engine has been fitted with a rather clumsy extended smokebox and appears to have simplified lining below the platform, possibly vermilion only.   *Author's collection*

the corresponding position to the right. Characters were sans-serif in gold, and the shading colour is reported as being 'red', shadowed in black. However, class marking changed at some point; originally, each door was marked in the waist with a medium-sized numeral followed by an underlined abbreviation, for example "3$^{\underline{RD}}$" or "1$^{\underline{ST}}$", but by the end of 1906 large seriffed numerals were being applied to the lower door panels. The shading colours on these numerals, and apparently on the other lettering, were blue to the left and vermilion below, shadowed in black. This may actually be an indication of the earlier shading as well. It is not known how long this style had been in use. It also seems that lining was abandoned at the same time.

The LD&ECR had a number of non-passenger vehicles but their livery is not recorded. Following the practice of other railways, it is likely they were painted in an unlined version of the carriage 'lake'.

Although the *Locomotive Magazine* of December 1906 alludes to 'chocolate', it is generally accepted that goods wagons were grey, with black below the solebar. When new, body ironwork was painted black, but this may not have been retained in traffic. Lettering was in large white letters "LDEC" about 15 inches high, occupying the upper planks of open wagons, and between the framing of vans and cattle wagons. The wagon number was placed at the lower right. Tare was in italic characters on the left of the bottom rail. Brake vans are recorded as being varnished wood, with vermilion bufferbeams.

There was one group of wagons that were lettered in an unusual style, and it is believed that these were the leased coal wagons, of which there were quite a number. While the letters "L D E C" were used as before, they sloped backwards to the left. The wagons also carried other lettering, for example "TO CARRY 10 TONS" and "FOR COAL TRAFFIC".

1	'VERMILION' CARTER 36 PANTONE 485 BS 5252 04 E 55 OR BS 381 536 'POPPY RED'	**2**	'CRIMSON LAKE' CARTER 28 PANTONE 188 BS 381 540 'CRIMSON'

Manchester, Sheffield & Lincolnshire Railway

In 1836 a body of leading businessmen in Sheffield and Manchester formed the Sheffield, Ashton-under-Lyne & Manchester Railway, formally incorporated in 1837. The route was a bold one, penetrating the Pennines with the Woodhead Tunnel, which when opened in December 1845 was the longest tunnel in the world. In Manchester the SA&MR shared London Road station jointly with what was soon to become the London & North Western Railway. The Manchester, Sheffield & Lincolnshire Railway was formed in 1847 by the amalgamation of the SA&MR with the Great Grimsby & Sheffield Junction Railway (authorised 1845), the Sheffield & Lincolnshire Railway (authorised 1847) and the Great Grimsby Dock Company. The Lincolnshire lines were opened in 1849.

The MS&LR was essentially a west to east line, hemmed in by potentially hostile rivals. Under the guidance of Edward Watkin, General Manager 1854-61 and Chairman 1864-94, a policy of expansion by joint lines was pursued with the L&NWR, the Great Northern Railway, the North Staffordshire Railway and the Midland Railway. The largest joint achievement was the Cheshire Lines Committee formed with the GNR in 1865 and admitting the MR in 1866. This gave access to Liverpool, Lancashire, Cheshire and the Wirral.

Watkin's greatest ambition was an extension to London to meet up with his other railways, the Metropolitan, East London and South Eastern, to create a through route via a tunnel under the English Channel to Paris. After several attempts and much opposition the London Extension Act was passed in March 1893 and the die was cast for the MS&LR, renamed the Great Central Railway in August 1897, to become a trunk line (see p. 111).

Please note, if readers would like to research the Manchester Sheffield & Lincolnshire Railway section in *Britain's Railway Liveries* (E.F. Carter) for themselves, that some of the paragraphs quoted from *Moore's Monthly Magazine* in 1896 which deal with the passenger and goods stock livery have been erroneously printed as the first paragraph of the Lancashire, Derbyshire & East Coast Railway section.

Under Charles Sacré (1859-86), Manchester, Sheffield & Lincolnshire Railway locomotives were painted 'Brunswick green' with reddish-brown underframes, which at the time were almost invariably outside frames. These colours were undoubtedly very similar to those later introduced to the Great Central Railway by Mr J.G. Robinson. Small panels like splashers, sand boxes, spring buckles and tender flares were edged with black and a fine white line between it and the green. Corners on sandboxes were incurved. Boiler bands were black edged in white, cab fronts and dome bases being lined in the same way. Cab sides, tank sides and tenders were edged with a wide black band, having a vermilion line with incurved corners between the black and the body colour. Inside the

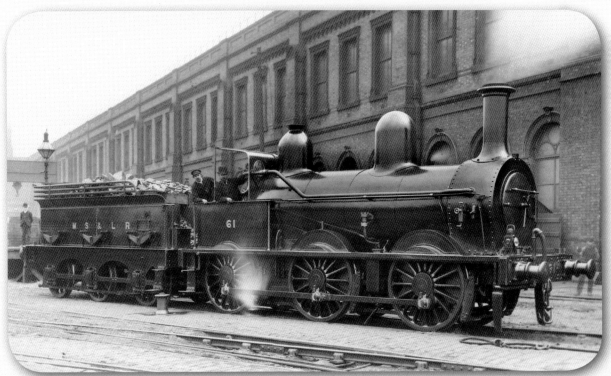

Sacré Class '18' 0-6-0 No. 61 carrying the later Parker livery circa 1890. Note the broad border of black and how faintly the emulsion registers the orange-yellow lining   Author's collection

vermilion line a white line was placed to form a wide band of green. Tender sides were lined out in a single panel, except where vertical riveting and strapping intervened, when the lining was in two or three panels. Latterly, it seems that rivets were ignored and single panels were more usual.

The red-brown underfames were lined with a thin line of vermilion placed a small distance from the edges. Buffer beams were also red-brown, edged with a vermilion line, a round-ended panel of vermilion being between the buffers, edged with a white line. Outside cranks were often vermilion, as were coupling rods of goods and mixed-traffic engines.

Locomotives allocated to the top passenger links were further embellished by an additional white line on each side of the boiler bands, inside the white lining of the smaller panels, and inside the vermilion lining on the frames. Where the frames had holes close to the edges, this involved the white lines combining into one for the necessary distance.

Numberplates were large and elliptical in brass. An outer band carried "MS&L" (or "SYR" for locomotives from the leased South

The Sacré locomotive livery and numberplate.

NIGEL J. L. DIGBY 1997

Yorkshire Railway) at the top, with "R^Y[date]C^O" below. The ellipse inside carried only the engine number in seriffed numerals. The background of the outer band was painted vermilion, the central part being blue. However, there may be a case from photographs that latterly the backgrounds were entirely blue. There was no other lettering on locomotives.

Mr Sacré resigned in 1886 to be replaced by Thomas Parker as Locomotive, Carriage & Wagon Superintendent. Mr Parker simplified the livery by abandoning the elaborate Sacré lining. Body colour was still Brunswick green, and outside frames, valances, step plates and buffers remained red-brown. Wheels were green with black tyres and axle ends, and inside frames and guard irons were black. The inner faces of the frames, the motion, and the buffer beams were vermilion. Inside the cab was 'stone colour'.

Boiler bands were black, and splashers, cab sides, tank sides and tenders were edged with a wide border of black, the edging having ordinary curved corners. Between the black and the green was a fine line of orange-yellow, made up from a mixture of white, chrome yellow and venetian red. The red-brown areas had a narrow black edging lined in orange-yellow. Wheel tyres and centres were also lined.

Brass numberplates were abandoned and numbers were transferred on cab sides, with "M S & L R" on tank and tender sides. The figures and characters were sans-serif in gold shaded to right and below with red, picked out with white. Driving wheel splashers of express engines carried the MS&LR armorial device. Buffer beams carried "N^O" and the number in gold, shaded black, and were edged in black and yellow.

The armorial device consisted of a circular arrangement of the shields of the five principal towns and cities served by the railway, surrounded by a garter containing the words "MANCHESTER SHEFFIELD & LINCOLNSHIRE".

Harry Pollitt took over from Mr Parker in 1894 and presided over the change from MS&LR to GCR. At the end of Mr Parker's period and during Mr Pollitt's sojourn the Brunswick green was lightened. Outside frames and valances were now 'brown', but ordinary inside frames were now common and these were simply black. On passenger engines brown was applied to the portion of frames above the footplate forming the smokebox saddle. Buffer casings and guard irons were also brown. The wheel tyres of express engines were polished steel, and the armorial device was carried as before.

This was essentially the livery used by the Great Central until about 1901, the words "GREAT CENTRAL" being substituted for "MS&LR", in the same sans-serif lettering. A new registered coat of arms replaced the MS&LR device.

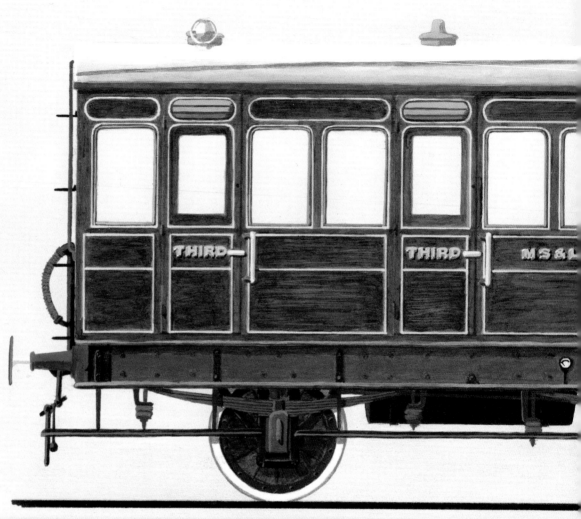

Parker Class '9F' 0-6-2T No. 745, built by Beyer, Peacock & Co. in 1893. An elegant engine in a simple livery.

Author's collection

Coaches up to 1857 were 'claret' or crimson, but thereafter and for the remainder of the MS&LR period were varnished teak. Mr Parker designed the carriages to rather resemble a compound of vehicles from the Great Eastern and Great Northern railways. The top quarter panels and the quarter lights were beaded in the conventional way, the upper corners of the windows being curved, but cut at right angles at the bottom. However, on the waist and lower body were applied rectangles of half-round beading. Carriage lining was gold around the upper mouldings, and along the centre of the beading on and below the waist. Roofs and wheel tyres were white when first out of shops.

There is reason to believe that, in common with other railways with teak carriages, after a period of time they were painted teak colour. The company minutes of 3rd July 1896 reveal that the MS&LR preferred the name 'Old Oak Brown'.

The treatment of solebars is somewhat in question. In *Moore's Monthly Magazine* it was stated that solebars were painted and grained to a lighter shade of brown than the body, and ironwork

was 'bronzed green'. However, the MS&LR also specified the construction of carriages destined for the Cheshire Lines (see Volume Three), almost certainly simply using their own standard specification. In this, solebars were entirely painted green, then 'bronze painted', followed by finishing varnish. It may well be that this was simply the method used on bogie carriages with steel underframes, rather than the simpler method used for 4- and 6-wheel carriages with wooden underframes.

Lettering was in plain block characters 3 inches high in gold, blocked in blue and shaded in black. Class marking was in words on each door, including Second Class until 1891, or 1892 in the Manchester area. The standard layout for 6-wheeled coaches with four compartments (Firsts, Seconds, Composites) was apparently a central "MS&L", flanked on each side by the number having an armorial device below. Five-compartment Thirds seem not to have had the device, with "MS&L" in the waist to the left, the number to the right. Saloons were given two groups of lettering, for example "MS&L No1033" with a device below each.

Horseboxes and other non-passenger vehicles were painted a 'light umber brown', which is a typical layman's phrase printed in the railway press. It was probably the standard railway 'teak colour' to match the wood of the coaches. Lettering was in yellow, shaded in blue and black.

As far as is known, wagons were always a light medium grey, including solebars. Below the solebars everything was black. Lettering was plain, in white 6-inch block letters with "MS&L" to the upper left and the number to the upper right. Load was marked in 2-inch characters on the bottom right-hand plank. The number appeared again in about 3-inch figures on the left of the solebar, with the tare to the right. Near the centre of the solebar was a five-pointed star, about 4½ inches across, which seems to be one of those symbols used by several railways in the earlier period.

The five-pointed star appeared again on the wagon sheets in yellow. The sheets were also marked "MS&L", apparently in about 18-inch seriffed letters along both sides, and had unspecified red and yellow stripes, possibly in a diagonal cross.

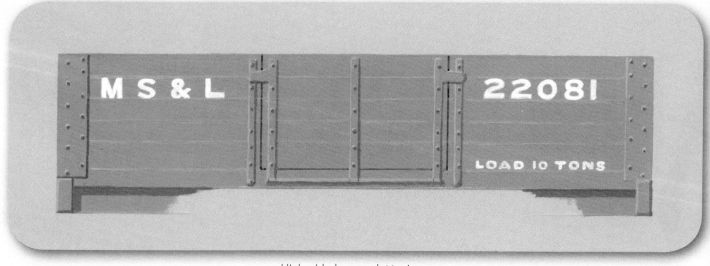

High-sided wagon lettering.

Midland & Great Northern Joint Railway

The Midland & Great Northern Joint Railways Committee was Britain's largest joint railway with 183 route miles, plus a further 23 jointly with the Great Eastern Railway. Its route was across country from Peterborough and Bourne to Yarmouth, Norwich and Cromer via King's Lynn. The section west of Lynn was largely in place by 1866, whilst the section east of Lynn was an amalgamation of two local Norfolk lines (the Lynn & Fakenham Railway and the Yarmouth & North Norfolk Railway), started in 1876 and built towards each other until they eventually met in 1883. The Eastern & Midlands Railway was formed in that year and owned the whole system east and west of King's Lynn. The western section was worked by the Great Northern and Midland railways, leaving the eastern section to be worked with E&MR locomotives and stock. The MR and the GNR assumed joint control of the lines west of King's Lynn in 1889, but the E&MR got into difficulties, a receiver being appointed in 1890. The two joint partners expressed an interest in acquiring the whole railway, and in July 1893 the Midland & Great Northern Joint Railways Committee was incorporated.

The 'Joint', as it was widely known, had its headquarters in King's Lynn, but its engineering works (and paint shop) were at Melton Constable. The M&GN remained unchanged by the Grouping of 1923, remaining jointly-owned by the London Midland & Scottish Railway and London & North Eastern Railway, but was worked entirely by the L&NER from October 1936. It passed into the Eastern Region of British Railways in 1948.

Locomotive livery of the Lynn & Fakenham Railway and the Yarmouth & North Norfolk Railway was specified as 'green to pattern' and 'red-brown to pattern' on an order for Beyer, Peacock, who built the Class 'A' 4-4-0s for the L&FR from 1882. The green has been described as similar to that of the Great Central Railway, in essence a medium chrome green. Boiler clothing, body panels and wheels were green, but valances, cylinders, inside frames and tender frames were red-brown. Smokeboxes, cab roofs, platforms (footplates), wheel tyres, tops of tanks and all the usual areas such as brake gear were black. Motion, axles and inside faces of frames were vermilion, as were safety valve levers and bufferbeams, including buffer casings. All lining was in black, fine-lined with white. Engines were named with brass plates having a vermilion background.

The only exceptions to the green livery were the ex-Cornwall Minerals Railway engines bought secondhand, which apparently retained their existing livery of brown, lined in black and yellow. The first three were given names and bore numbers in brass on the front of the chimney, but the remaining five retained their CMR

M&GN Class 'C' 4-4-0 No. 53 as rebuilt in 1910 with large G7 boiler, Deeley cab and enclosed splashers. The wheels have been shown erroneously in light brown rather than burnt sienna. *Author's collection*

numbers on rectangular brass plates in the centre of the tanks, "Nᵒ 12" for example. When the Class 'A' 4-4-0s arrived, they had elliptical brass numberplates on the cabside and no names, which became the later standard. The background to the numberplates was vermilion, as was the background to the curved Beyer, Peacock maker's plate over the driving wheels.

The Eastern & Midlands Railway adopted brown for their livery (see title page). The whole engine, including frames, wheels and valances was middle brown. Smokeboxes, cab roofs, platforms, tank and tender tops, and wheel tyres were black. Lining was in black and yellow, probably lemon chrome. Body panels were edged in black, fine-lined yellow, and boiler bands, outside cylinders, tanks and tenders were lined with bands of black, also fine-lined yellow. Bufferbeams and buffer casings were vermilion [1], lined in black only. Motion, axles and the inner faces of frames were also vermilion.

Nameplates were removed (except from two small contractor's engines) and numbers applied. The Class 'B' 4-4-0Ts had only bufferbeam numbers in the usual format, for example "Nᵒ [hook] 9", while the ex-CMR engines and the several saddletanks possessed by the railway had numbers painted on the tanks. Only the Class 'A' 4-4-0s had elliptical numberplates as standard when they were delivered, until eventually the other engines started receiving them from about 1890.

Company lettering appeared on tenders and the tanks of the Class 'B' 4-4-0Ts, in gold 6-inch characters, shaded in black. The early lettering was "E & M Rʸ", but from the time of the introduction of the armorial device in 1890, lettering became standardised as "E & [device] M R".

When the Midland & Great Northern Joint Railways Committee was created in 1893, the locomotive stock inherited from the E&MR was expanded by batches of Midland-designed 4-4-0s (Class 'C') and 0-6-0s (Class 'D') delivered between 1894 and 1899, and a batch of GNR-designed 0-6-0s (Class 'DA') in 1901. Melton Constable also built and rebuilt further locomotives.

During the first months of the new organisation, it seems clear that Melton Constable expected the livery colour to remain the E&MR middle brown, as it was specified in December 1893 that the ten engines to be built by Sharp, Stewart (the first of the Class 'C' 4-4-0s) were to be the same colour as the engines taken over by the Joint Committee. However, the decision was taken to change the colour while the locomotives were being built. The M&GN locomotive colour, often described as yellow but in fact light brown [2], had no official name. It was known variously as 'iron hydrate', 'Quaker green' or (in the paint shop) 'autumn leaf'. Before the First World War, upon the lead colour undercoat, it was built up from the applications of two coats of yellow ochre, one coat of raw sienna, then three coats of varnish. It was the glazing coat

NIGEL J. L. DIGBY 1996

of transparent raw sienna that added the darker greenish brown tint to the yellow ochre beneath. During the 1920s, the method was simplified by mixing yellow ochre, burnt umber and burnt sienna to a colour card, but the hue remained the same. Further specifications and methods of M&GN painting can be found in Volume One.

Light brown was applied to all above the platform, except for the smokebox, cab roof, splasher tops, tender and tank tops, which were black. Valances, outside cylinders, frames and wheels were burnt sienna [3], a red brown natural earth colour referred to as 'chocolate' in the paint shop. Burnt sienna was also used on the beading dividing MR-type tenders into two panels, and as a strip at top and bottom of the tenders of the GNR-type 0-6-0s. All lining on both light brown and burnt sienna areas was in black and lemon chrome. Tanks, tenders, splashers and other panels were bordered in 1-inch of black, fine-lined on the inside with lemon chrome.

Example of lettering incorporating the device as seen on the tenders of the Class 'A' 4-4-0s and Class 'DA' 0-6-0s, and the tanks of the Class 'B' 4-4-0Ts.

Cab sides, tanks and tenders were lined with 1½-inch black bands. Boiler bands were also black. All this black lining was fine-lined on both sides with ¼-inch of lemon chrome to make bands 2 inches in width.

Wheel tyres were black edged with lemon chrome, and wheel centres were lined in two rings of black and lemon chrome, the yellow being on the inner edge only. Cab interiors were a painted and grained 'oak' finish above toolbox level, and black below. Safety valve levers, motion and frame interiors were vermilion. Buffer beams were also vermilion, edged with a plain black line, there also being a black outer lip to the buffer casings. Many of the smaller tank engines had vermilion coupling rods.

At first there were several experiments on E&MR engines with the lettering, using the sans-serif characters, often in the form "M & G N J R" or even "M & G [device] N J R", but once again Melton Constable was overruled. Lettering was to be in the Midland style, being seriffed in gold, shaded in blue, dark blue and white and shadowed in black. Thanks to a request from the Railway Clearing House, the first batch of Midland-type Class 'C' 4-4-0s delivered in 1894 were lettered "J^T M & G N R", but the style therefter was

simply "M & G N", also applied to the tenders of the Class 'D' 0-6-0s. The armorial device appeared on the driving wheel splashers of both classes.

The Class 'B' 4-4-0T engines, and the plain-sided tenders of the Class 'A' 4-4-0s and Class 'DA' 0-6-0s had the device centrally between the lettering "M & [device] G N". The 0-6-0T shunting tanks 'rebuilt' from the Cornwall Mineral Railway engines at Melton Constable had a central numberplate, so the lettering was disposed on each side, for example "M & (93) G N", and the device was placed above the numberplate. Buffer beams of all engines carried the usual lettering, for example "N^O [hook] 53", in gold, blue and black.

An exception to this standardisation was seen on the three Class 'A Tank' 4-4-2Ts built at Melton Constable, which had "MIDLAND & GREAT NORTHERN" in 6-inch gold lettering shaded in black, arranged in an arc above the device. The device itself had a diamond-shaped lozenge of lining around it. This decoration also appeared on the various large boiler rebuilds of Class 'C' 4-4-0s and Class 'D' 0-6-0s, although the first two 4-4-0s rebuilt in 1908 had a shield shape instead.

The device was inherited from the E&MR and consisted of the arms of Norwich, Yarmouth, Peterborough and Lynn quartered on a decorated shield within a white garter. On the garter the name "EASTERN & MIDLANDS RAILWAY." was superseded by "MIDLAND & GREAT NORTHERN JOINT RAILWAY." in black sans-serif letters. From 1910 the garter became blue with gold lettering.

Numberplates used at Melton Constable up to 1907 were elliptical brass, 16 x 11 inches, with raised numbers and vermilion backgrounds. However, engines from the parent companies had the Midland 6½-inch brass cut-out numerals. Rebuilds and construction at Melton from 1908 also used brass numerals in the Midland style, but increased in size to 9 inches.

Passenger vehicles were originally only those inherited from the E&MR and its constituents, and these, being built from mahogany on oak framing, were finished in a painted and grained teak imitation throughout their lives. Lining was in ¼-inch lemon chrome around the mouldings, fine-lined with ultramarine blue. Many more carriages were purchased from the MR and GNR in 1903, and at first these were relettered on their original liveries (crimson and

teak respectively), but on their first repaint the ex-Midland vehicles were all finished in the teak graining. The varnished natural teak of the ex-GNR vehicles was retained, and as further transferals from the GNR resulted in them becoming the largest component of the stock, varnished teak was soon seen as the official carriage finish. These vehicles were also lined in lemon chrome edged in blue. Solebars were teak colour [5], with bronzed metalwork, and all metalwork below the solebars was black. Wood-centred Mansell wheels were varnished teak or painted teak colour.

Carriage lettering retained a similar appearance throughout the E&MR and early M&GN periods. Lettering was in the waist panels in 4-inch gold sans-serif characters, with class marking on the doors in words, "FIRST" or "THIRD", the initial letter being 4-inch but the rest of the word in 3-inch characters. On the smaller 4-wheel carriages, the company initials "E&MR" appeared to the left and the number to the right. On the larger 6-wheel carriages, the initials were central, with two numbers placed symmetrically towards each end. The device was placed centrally on Thirds, or on each First Class door of Composites. It is believed that the gold characters were shaded with blue and white, shadowed in black.

At the start of the M&GN period, the initials "JᵀM&GN" (as requested by the RCH) were substituted, but the other arrangements were unaltered. It is possible that the shading colour during this early period may have been red as used by the Midland Railway, but this is unconfirmed. By about 1898 the "Jᵀ" had been dropped and plain "M&GN" was being used routinely. With the influx of the secondhand carriages purchased from the MR and GNR in 1903 some were lettered thus, complete with class wording, but no device.

From about 1904 a new standard style was evolved, centred on the middle door of the vehicle, being "MIDLAND & [door] Gᵀ NORTHERN" in 3 inch sans-serif gold characters, with large 9-inch class numbers on the lower panels of the doors. The device was no longer used on rolling stock. The shading colour to the lettering was now dark blue, light blue and white, shadowed in black. Numbers on most carriages were placed two on each side in a symmetrical arrangement. Some vehicles such as certain Composites and Saloons had only four doors on each side and these were lettered "M&GN" on the left-hand panel between two doors, and the number in a corresponding position to the right.

Luggage vans were lettered "M&GN" and "LUGGAGE VAN" on the available panels, and the ex-GNR vehicles had their number actually on the upper body panels.

Non-passenger carriage stock such as horseboxes and carriage trucks received the same painted and grained teak finish as used on the passenger stock. They were given a limited amount of lining in lemon chrome, and lettered in sans-serif characters in the same colour. Interiors were stone colour.

Throughout the E&MR and M&GN periods, revenue goods wagons were painted brown oxide [6], the same wagon colour as on the Great Northern Railway. The original owning company lettered its open wagons "L&FRʸ", earning it the nickname 'Liver and Fry'. The unified railway substituted "E&MRʸ", but by 1890 were using "EASTERN & MIDLANDS RAILWAY" in full along the top plank.

On the creation of the joint committee, open wagons were originally lettered "JᵀM&GN" with the ampersand positioned centrally on the body. The lettering was in white and placed along the top plank of low-sided wagons, and on the top two planks of high-sided examples, with the numbers to the lower right. Vans

Standard open goods wagon livery.

and cattle wagons had the number incorporated with the lettering along the centre line of the crossed outside framing, for example "JT [X] M&[doors]GN [X] 550". Tare was in italic numerals on the left-hand side of the bottom rail. There were no numberplates, the company initials and number simply being painted in small characters on the solebar.

By 1900 the simple "M&GN" lettering had been adopted. At first it still tended to be painted on the top two planks of high-sided open wagons, but it soon assumed a more normal position on the middle two planks (all M&GN high-sided wagons were four planks high). Lettering was generally in white and in various sizes: open wagons had 16-inch letters, cattle wagons 12-inch and vans 10-inch letters. Numbers were now to the lower left on open wagons, but on the upper right on vans and cattle wagons, which had outside framing. A numberplate was adopted, with incurved corners similar to that of the Midland, but smaller, being 11¼ x 7¾ inches. They were cast with "JTM&GN" above and the number below, in white letters on black.

Unlike the rest of the stock, M&GN brake vans were lettered in lemon chrome, and had 8-inch initials along the upper part of the body, with "10 TON BRAKE" below on the central part of the body in 4-inch characters, and a 6-inch number to bottom right. A handful of vans were rebuilt as 15-ton vehicles, their lettering being altered accordingly.

Service vehicles were painted red oxide and lettered "M & G N" in white. Their function was often added in small letters on the middle of the body, and all service vehicles carried a cast iron plate 19¼ x 2½ inches in size, painted black, with "RAILWAY SERVICE VEHICLE" picked out in white.

On the introduction of the common-user agreement in 1917, open wagons and unfitted vans were left the standard paint shop lead colour, a medium grey when going through shops. At this point, it seems that body numbering was abandoned on open wagons.

There is little information about wagon sheets. The commonest design apparently carried a diagonal white cross, with white corners. The initials "M&GN" with the number below were placed on each side, and probably also at each end in a smaller size.

After the Grouping of 1923, the M&GN remained a separate entity until Nationalisation, and although it is outside the general remit of 'pre-Grouping liveries' it would be absurd not to include

M&GN standard brake van livery.

what happened subsequently, and after the operational take-over by the L&NER in October 1936.

From 1922, the 0-6-0 tender engines of Classes 'D' and 'DA' were painted dark brown [4]. This was burnt umber enriched with burnt sienna. Lining on the Class 'D' 0-6-0s was simplified to ¼-inch lemon chrome lines, and their tenders were lined in a single rectangle ignoring the central vertical strip. In contrast, the Class 'DA' 0-6-0s were left completely unlined. Lettering on the dark brown was slightly larger than formerly at 9 inches, in a sans-serif style painted in lemon chrome. The device was no longer used. Buffer beams on these engines now carried only the number to the right of the drawhook, although the plain black edging was still used.

From 1929 the other locomotives were painted dark brown as they went through shops, lined simply in lemon chrome. A number of Class 'C' 4-4-0s still had the device applied on the dark brown, but this practice soon ceased. Lettering was increased to 12 inches, in new seriffed lemon chrome characters, also applied to the goods engines when they were repainted. The lemon chrome, under the influence of varnish, cleaning with tallow, and time, noticeably turned from yellow into a light orange colour.

All buffer beams now simply had the number to the right of the drawhook, with plain black lining as before. A few of the older

engines, including the two surviving Class 'B' 4-4-0Ts, were withdrawn in the early 1930s still carrying the light brown.

In October 1936, the L&NER immediately put all locomotives on the duplicate list and had a zero placed in front of the number. Many engines had the old cabside brass numerals removed and their new number applied in large hand-painted lemon chrome figures on the dark brown livery. Eventually the L&NER issued the order to begin painting M&GN locomotives black. A few were thus painted at Melton Constable in late 1936, but after the closure of the works in December the remainder were handled at Stratford (the Great Eastern Railway's old works). The Class 'A' 4-4-2Ts, Class 'C' 4-4-0s and Class 'D' 0-6-0s were considered mixed traffic and lined in vermilion, but Class 'DA' 0-6-0s and the shunting tanks were unlined black. Only one Class 'A' 4-4-0 remained in traffic (No. 25), and was also lined. Tenders carried the standard large "L N E R" transfers. As usual, the smaller size was used on tanksides, the number placed below.

The standard M&GN style of carriage painting managed to survive the Grouping, but by the 1930s the L&NER influence was being felt. All blue fine-lining was dropped around 1930, and from 1932 the full L&NER styling was adopted. Lettering was now in seriffed gold characters 4-inches high, shaded in dark red, light red and white, shadowed in black and brown. The

Late period M&GN locomotive lettering 1929-36, showing slight orange cast after time and cleaning with tallow.

M&GN late period carriage lettering and lining 1932-48.

arrangement was simplified to "M&GN" and the number in the waist, with large 9-inch seriffed class numerals on the lower doors. A great many vehicles were transferred from the LM&SR and L&NER, being of London & North Western, Midland, North Eastern and Great Eastern Railway origins, and this was the lettering they received. Some survivors were still carrying it in 1950.

From the 1920s, non-passenger stock was painted teak colour, but lettered and lined in lemon chrome in the same way as before. In 1928 all revenue goods stock was divided between the LM&SR and L&NER, leaving only the brake vans and service stock in M&GN livery. Brake vans were brown oxide until their withdrawal in the 1940s, and service stock remained red oxide, even those units which managed to survive into the 1950s.

M&GN Class 'A' 4-4-2T No. 9, showing curved tankside lettering and lozenge around the device. Built at Melton Constable March 1910, although officially a 'rebuild'. Once again the wheels are shown as light brown instead of burnt sienna, and there should be no white lining on the bufferbeam.   *Author's collection*

1 'VERMILION'
CARTER 36
PANTONE 485
BS 5252 04 E 55
OR BS 381 536
'POPPY RED'

2 'LIGHT BROWN'
CARTER 32
PANTONE 1395
BS 381 410
'LIGHT BROWN'

3 'BURNT SIENNA'
CARTER 44
PANTONE 175
RAL 8015
'CHESTNUT BROWN'

4 'DARK BROWN'
CARTER 39
PANTONE 476
BS 5252 06 C 40
OR RAL 8017
'CHOCOLATE BROWN'

5 'TEAK COLOUR'
CARTER 41
PANTONE 1615
BS 381 489
'LEAF BROWN'

6 'BROWN OXIDE'
CARTER 29
PANTONE 483
BS 381 448
'DEEP INDIAN RED'

❧ Mid-Suffolk Light Railway ❧

At the end of the 19th century, the rural district of 'High Suffolk' found itself surrounded by, yet not served by, the Great Eastern Railway. With the passing of the 1896 Light Railways Act an opportunity arose to open up the district to rail. This Act was meant to be one method of alleviating the agricultural depression then current, allowing railways to be built to a lesser standard than main lines, authorised by a Light Railway Order rather than the expensive rigmarole of an Act of Parliament.

The first public meeting was held in July 1899 and the Light Railway Order was issued in April 1900. The 'Middy', as it was affectionately known, was ambitiously planned, joining the GER at three places. The main line was to leave Haughley, heading north-west and passing through Mendlesham and Laxfield to Halesworth; a branch was to leave the main line at Kenton and turn south through Debenham to Westerfield near Ipswich.

There were problems raising capital, and construction was not begun until March 1902. By July 1904, the line had reached Cratfield, 6 miles from Halesworth, but there construction halted. Only 1½ miles of the Westerfield branch had been built. Opening for goods followed in September 1904, but the financial situation

was desperate and no money was available for further construction. Worse still, the Board of Trade Inspector refused to pass the line for passenger traffic in July 1905. Finally, the company was declared bankrupt in 1906, and a Receiver appointed.

An attempt to revive the Halesworth extension failed in 1907, and from this time the Westerfield branch was quietly forgotten. The good news was that on reinspection in 1908, the line was passed for passenger working, which begun on the 29th September. Further powers for the Halesworth extension were granted in 1909, but in 1912 it was finally abandoned.

The 'Middy' was absorbed into the London & North Eastern Railway in 1924, the delay being caused by difficulties addressing the company's liabilities, and passed into the Eastern Region of British Railways in 1948.

The Mid-Suffolk Light Railway owned three locomotives, all built by Hudswell, Clarke & Co. of Leeds. They were 0-6-0T engines of similar design, No. 1 arriving in 1904, No. 2 in 1905, and No. 3 in 1909. They were turned out in crimson, described as 'crimson lake' and 'dark red' – which was, incidentally, the standard for Hudswell, Clarke engines, unless otherwise specified. No. 1 and

Mid-Suffolk Light Railway 0-6-0T locomotives No. 3 and No. 2 at Stratford, probably just after Grouping. Engine No. 3 is running here as a 2-4-0T, its front coupling rods being removed. Engine No. 2 made it out of Stratford in glossy black paint as L&NER Class 'J64' No. 8317, and No. 1 became No. 8316, but No. 3 never ran again.
Author's collection

No. 3 were virtually identical, but No. 2 was slightly smaller and had its front sand boxes mounted above the footplate rather than below. All three were fitted with the Westinghouse automatic brake, the pumps being mounted on the offside of the smokebox. They were all placed on the line facing Laxfield, allowing them to be at their best when tackling the steep 1 in 42 gradient out of Haughley, there being no turntable.

The crimson body panels, valances and steps were bordered with black, and there was a black line separating the main part of the side tanks and bunker from the cab area. Most of the corners of this approximately 2-inch wide black band were incurved. Between the black and the body colour were thin lines of vermilion. About 1½ to 2 inches inside this border, and following its outline, was a thin yellow line. The distance between the vermilion and yellow lines on the valances and steps was smaller, perhaps 1 inch. Boiler bands were black, edged in vermilion, with yellow lines on each side painted on the boiler cleading plates. Wheel tyres were black edged in vermilion, and the axle ends appear to have been black, lined with yellow, although it is difficult to tell from photographs.

Bufferbeams were vermilion, edged in black and apparently lined in white, as it appears more prominent in photographs than the yellow lining. The ends of the buffer casings were also black, lined in white. The number was applied in the usual fashion, for example "Nᵒ [hook] 3" in gold seriffed characters shaded in black. Numbers were also carried on an elliptical plate on the bunker, bordered by "MID-SUFFOLK LIGHT RAILWAY Cᵒ" in polished brass on a vermilion background. Domes, safety valves and safety valve seatings were polished brass, and the chimney caps were polished copper, although taller plain chimneys were fitted to No. 1 and No. 2 in 1920 and 1921. There was also a brass fillet between the boiler and the smokebox.

The company initials "M S L R" appeared on the tanks in gold letters, shaded in a colour and highlighted in white. The colour has a dark appearance on photographs and was probably vermilion. The design of the sans-serif characters was unusual, particularly the "M" whose central downstrokes did not reach the baseline, contrary to all good railway practice. This leads me to believe that the letters were hand-applied rather than standard transfers.

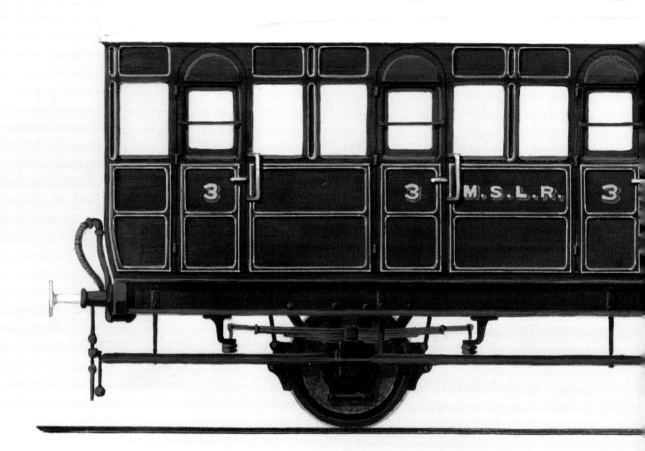

Carriages were all 4-wheel and obtained secondhand. Passenger brake No. 1 was an ex-GER vehicle, purchased in 1904 and converted from an 1875 Brake Third, but the remaining seven were all ex-Metropolitan. These were built between 1887 and 1892, and were modified by G.R. Turner of Nottingham before being delivered in 1905. Originally they ran in two close-coupled sets of three, but from the end of 1911 the close-coupled sets were separated to allow individual working, and full-length buffers replaced the old short ones where appropriate.

Carriages were painted crimson to match the locomotives. Roofs were originally white, and solebars and footboards probably black. Body mouldings were lined with yellow and fine-lined with vermilion. Lettering was in gold sans-serif characters, apparently shaded in vermilion and white. Class marking was in numerals on the waist panel of each door. Other lettering seems to have changed over time. As first delivered, the initials "M.S.L.R." (with stops) were placed to the left, between the first and second compartment doors, with the number placed in the corresponding position on

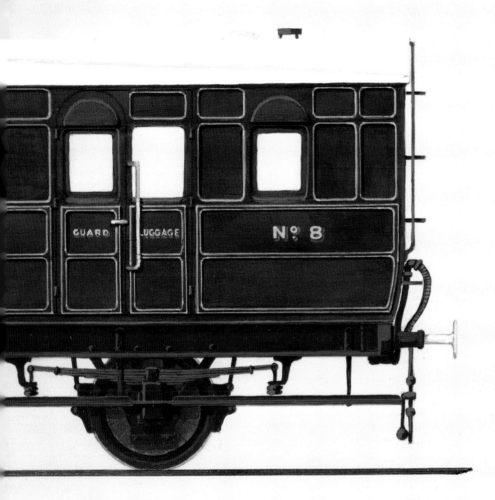

the right. A prefix was used at all times, for example "№ 2". After the carriages had received attention in 1912 the initials were moved to a central position, the numerals being placed at the extreme right, except for the Brake Thirds where there is evidence to suggest that the numbers on both sides of the vehicle were at the brake end. When the GER performed remedial work on the carriages at Ipswich from 1919, it seems that their transfers were used, at least for class marking; a photograph exists of part of one carriage showing a seriffed "3" on the door. The crimson then current on

GER carriages may also have been used for the body colour, being a close match.

There were two horseboxes, both ex-GER, and these were painted crimson, with limited yellow lining. They were lettered on the dropping part of the door, with "MID-SUFFOLK LIGHT" on one plank, "RAILWAY" on the plank below and the number (№ 9 and № 10) below that.

Goods stock consisted of four low drop-sided wagons, sixteen high-sided open wagons, six cattle wagons and two brake vans.

NIGEL J.L. DIGBY 2005

Wagons were painted a mid-grey, apparently a little lighter than the GER wagon colour, with black below the solebar. Iron strapping on the body was painted black, one of the few instances of this practice actually being maintained in traffic. Lettering was distinctive. On the open wagons, the name "MID SUFFOLK" was painted in bold white 12-inch letters along the top planks of the side. The number, preceded by "Nº", was on the lower left plank in 6-inch characters, with the tare in 3-inch italics on the lower right. No numberplates were carried. Wagon No. 9 was converted into a van but the lettering remained undisturbed. Cattle wagons had less prominent markings, the wording being spaced out between the crossed framing in approximately 4-inch white letters. When new, these were shaded in black. "MID- [frame] SUFFOLK" appeared on the left and "TARE [frame] Nº19" on the right of the central doors. The tare was painted on the plank below the word, and "LARGE" was painted above the cross of the right-hand framing. When repainted by the Mid-Suffolk, letters were plain white, and the words "TARE" and "LARGE" were omitted, the tare being painted in italics in the corresponding space.

The brake vans were lettered differently. No. 1, an ex-GER vehicle, simply had "MID SUFFOLK" in the centre of the side, in about 3-inch letters, although the M and S were slightly larger. The number was painted above in 6-inch letters. The second brake, built new for the railway and based on a Midland design, was lettered more ambitiously, with "MID-SUFFOLK RY" along the upper body in about 9-inch lettering, "BRAKE VAN" below in 6-inch, and the number in 9-inch characters below that, all in white shaded in black.

It has been suggested that the cattle wagons and brake van No. 2 were painted brown. Nothing I have ever seen has convinced me that this is anything but apocryphal. It was not until the London & North Eastern Railway era that it became practice to paint brakes and fitted stock brown, which is perhaps being recalled here. Even so, merely through-piped vehicles such as the MSLR cattle wagons would not have been painted brown.

Wagon sheets, from what little can be discovered, were lettered "MID SUFFOLK" in white seriffed characters, probably on each long side with the number below.

❧ North British Railway ❧

The North British Railway was incorporated in 1844 for a line from Edinburgh to Berwick, and by amalgamation and absorption of over fifty other railways became the premier line in Scotland and fifth largest in Britain, with almost 1,378 route miles. The system evolved into a densely-packed network of lines between Edinburgh and Glasgow, and covering the counties of Kinross and Fife to the north and Peebles, Berwick and Roxburgh to the south. It reached down into England at Berwick and, via the famed 'Waverley Route' through Hawick, to Carlisle. It was a partner of the East Coast route and was responsible for the permanent way over the Forth Bridge, opened in 1890. Its most legendary constituent, the West Highland line, was opened to Fort William in 1894 and Mallaig in 1901.

The NBR's rival was the Caledonian Railway (Volume Three), but their relations seemed to veer regularly between antagonism and co-operation within the space of a few months. They nearly amalgamated in 1871, but this was rejected in the following year. Their rivalry did not prevent them from participating in several joint lines together, the most important being the Forth Bridge railway mentioned above and the Dundee & Arbroath Joint along the east

coast of Scotland, enabling the North British to get to Aberdeen. The railway's works were at Cowlairs, in Glasgow.

In 1923 the North British became a constituent of the London & North Eastern Railway, and passed to the Scottish Region of British Railways in 1948.

The liveries of the line are still a contentious issue and the subject of research by the NBR Study Group, but there are known periods which can be generalized below.

The first recorded locomotive livery as used by locomotive superintendent Mr Thomas Wheatley (1867-74) was described as green, with Indian red frames. A significant change occurred after the appointment of Dugald Drummond (1875-82), who brought with him from his time at Brighton a version of Mr Stroudley's LB&SC livery, a light brown based on yellow ochre. The dark red framing and dark green edging were employed just as on the LB&SC, but the lining was slightly different, being black bordered with white on both sides. The naming of locomotives was also instituted.

The most long-lasting NBR livery was developed by Mr Matthew Holmes (1882-1903) from the Drummond style circa 1885; it

North British Railway Class 'K' 4-4-0 No. 865 built at Cowlairs in 1909 pilots an unidentified 0-6-0 on a West Highland line express through Glenfinnan station. The treatment of the front bufferbeam can be clearly seen.

Author's collection

was used, with slight alterations, until the Grouping. Mr Holmes darkened the original light yellow-brown locomotive colour to a brown ochre, containing a slight greenish hue [1]. The responses of contemporary observers show great confusion regarding how to describe this strange greenish-brown colour. The various attempts include 'olive green', 'dark brown', 'dark yellow', 'yellow-brown ochre', 'greenish-khaki', 'brownish olive' or 'deep khaki'. There was even a description of 'dark gamboge', which, although it sounds plausible, is actually nonsense as gamboge was a bright yellow pigment not used for oil colour. Contemporary postcards and coloured illustrations in the railway press invariably show a brown, rather than a green, although the patch in E.F. Carter's *Britain's Railway Liveries* is generally agreed to be slightly too brown.

The brown ochre colour was bordered by a dark green as before, described as 'Brunswick green'. The junction between the two colours was lined with black, bordered on the outer green side with vermilion [2] and inner brown side with yellow. At first the dark red valancing of the LB&SC-style livery was retained, but this had

been replaced with the main body colour by circa 1890. Lining below the footplate was in black and vermilion only, except for a ring of yellow around the black axle ends of the wheels. Boiler bands were black, edged with vermilion, with about a 2-inch band of dark green painted onto the boiler clothing on each side, edged with yellow.

Lettering was "N.B.R." with square full stops, in 6-inch gold letters shaded in red and highlighted in white, shadowed in black. Any names from the Drummond period were removed. Numberplates were elliptical brass, with "NORTH BRITISH" over and "RAILWAY" under the central number, all in sunken characters filled with black wax. An armorial device was applied to the splashers of passenger locomotives from 1893 onwards. The device consisted of the arms of Edinburgh and Berwick, originally inside a circlet bearing the title of the railway "THE NORTH BRITISH RAILWAY COMPANY.", but from about 1900 the circlet was replaced by a belted garter.

Forward bufferbeams were painted in the brown ochre body

NIGEL J. L. DIGBY 1994

colour bordered in black and fine-lined in vermilion, except for a central panel of vermilion between the buffers, which was outlined with yellow. Numbers were shown on this vermilion panel in the usual form, for example "Nº [hook] 239", in gold seriffed characters shaded in black. Buffer casings were brown, lined at the outer lip with black and yellow. Tender bufferbeams were left unadorned brown ochre.

Under the tenure of Mr William Paton Reid (1904-19) the lettering size was increased to 9 inches and the device was incorporated into the lettering on most locomotives, which became "N. [device] B." on tanks and tenders. From the introduction of Mr Reid's famous Class 'H' 4-4-2 Atlantics in 1906, a policy of naming the more important engines was again instituted. Names were in a small version of the standard lettering, about 4 inches high, following the upper curve of lining on the front splashers. The rear splashers of the Atlantics featured the armorial device, and so it was not needed on the tender, which simply carried "N.B.R".

However, the biggest change to the railway's livery that Mr Reid

presided over was the alteration of the brown ochre base colour to a much greener shade of brown known (perhaps a little misleadingly) as bronze green, which occurred about 1911. There were no other changes, the dark green edging and the vermilion panel on the front bufferbeam being retained. In my opinion, something like BS 4800 10 B 39 Seaweed – Pantone 4485 is in the right area.

Application of the new standard lettering incorporating the device was not necessarily universal, as for some reason the 1913 batch of Class 'A' 0-6-2Ts, built for the railway by the North British Locomotive Company, were delivered lettered "N.B.R.", in noticeably larger 12-inch initials.

After two years of the bronze green, in September 1913 a centralised traffic control system was adopted, and in order to help signalmen to identify the train engine, large 18-inch numerals began to take the place of the armorial device, for example "N.1404 B.". All sans-serif characters were still in the gold, shaded with red and white to the left, and shadowed in black to the right and below. At the same time, there were simplifications. Buffer beams were now

Example panel of 'bronze green' livery with large reporting numbers adopted 1913.

plain vermilion, edged in black and fine-lined in yellow, on which the engine number appeared in the conventional way, still in the seriffed characters.

The final change occurred at the end of 1914, from which time goods locomotives were painted black, lined only in yellow. Tenders, tanks, cabsides and splashers were lined with yellow lines in pairs, 2 inches apart, forming panels. Boiler bands were edged with yellow, and valances and tender frames had a single yellow line. Tender bufferbeams were plain black. Latterly, the "N.B." lettering also increased to 12 inches from its former 9 inches.

This was the situation when Mr William Chalmers became superintendent in 1919. It must be borne in mind that such rapid changes resulted in there being a great variety of styles in existence by 1923, with brown ochre engines rubbing shoulders with bronze green and black ones.

The method of making up the locomotive colour is very much in dispute. The Drummond LB&SCR-type livery was based on yellow ochre, and so too was the Holmes brown ochre. However, there are two reported methods of manufacturing the body colour. The first is a mixture of Quaker green, black and blue, the second is a mixture of burnt umber and Brunswick blue. From my past researches, despite what modern paint catalogues would have you believe, Quaker green was not green at all, but brown. It uses a late-18th century tendency to refer to anything Quaker as drab and

A contrast in Atlantics circa 1906. North Eastern Railway Class '4CC' Smith compound 4-4-2 No. 730, although the more powerful locomotive, is subdued by the massive presence of North British Railway Class 'H' 4-4-2 No. 868 Aberdonian, in standard brown ochre. The card was posted in December 1909.

Example panel of black goods locomotive livery adopted in 1914.

subdued, hence the rather ironic joke name of Quaker green for pigments like raw sienna or raw umber, which were greenish browns. Brunswick blue is Prussian blue extended with barytes. Neither of the two (unofficial) formulae is particularly satisfactory when tested by mixing the oil colours concerned. However, a combination of them using yellow ochre, burnt umber and Brunswick blue is much more flexible and can give a large range of shades from dark ochre to olive green. I would suggest therefore that there has been some confusion in the recording of these methods, but this is only a personal opinion.

There are three preserved locomotives of the North British Railway: 'Glen' Class 4-4-0 No. 256 *Glen Douglas*, Class 'C' 0-6-0 No. 673

Maude and Class 'G' 0-4-0ST No. 42. The 0-6-0 is appropriately painted in the post-1914 goods black, carrying the name given to it in 1919, but *Glen Douglas* is a little more problematic. It was built in 1913 and has been painted in the bronze green livery, which is at least correct, but surely to be fully representative of the period it should really have the large numerals on the tender rather than the device. The rear tender bufferbeam has also been treated with a vermilion panel in the same way as the front, which (as far as I understand it) is not correct. However, more seriously, the dark green edging to the body panels has been omitted, which in my view rather spoils the whole exercise. Perhaps the less said about 'pug' No. 42 the better.

Holmes Class 'M' 4-4-0 No. 36, carrying the post-1913 'bronze green' livery with large reporting numbers on the tender. The original print illustrates well the continued presence of the dark green borders to the panels and boiler bands.

Author's collection

Wagons were painted a light medium grey and a preserved sample of a wagon wrecked in an accident in 1917 suggests there was a greenish hue. Why this should be so is a mystery, and in the face of known paint shop practise does seem rather unlikely. New vehicles when photographed often had their body ironwork painted black, but in traffic it was painted the same colour as the body.

A quatrefoil in white was used as a distinctive North British symbol, as was the small white crescent containing the shop date. Until circa 1896 these were the only marks, but from that time the large white letters were introduced. Wagons were always lettered with the quatrefoil centrally "N [symbol] B", the initials being 18 inches on most stock, but reduced in size where space was limited. Vans had the quatrefoil placed as centrally as the door designs allowed. A rectangular numberplate with incurved corners was placed on the solebar, having "NORTH" over and "BRITISH" under the central number, picked out in white on a black background. Another feature of NB goods stock was the large label clip with spring retainer.

Brake vans were lettered in 6-inch characters on the upper side "N.B.R", with the number below, and "GOODS BRAKE" below that. Painted at the bottom of the side was the station to which the brake was allocated.

The exceptions to the grey wagon stock were the fitted 12-ton express goods vans, refrigerator vans, and fruit and yeast vans. These were brown, described in the railway press as Van Dyke brown mixed with chocolate. This was a typical layman's comment, citing a watercolour not used in oil and another indefinite subjective colour. It is possible, and even probable, that the colour involved was simply the base coat of the crimson vehicles, without the crimson glazing topcoats. It is therefore much more likely that the pigment was actually one of the iron oxides such as purple brown or brown oxide. Lettering on these vans was in yellow.

Wagon sheets were marked "N.B.R." on each side. The number was placed below preceded by a quatrefoil.

1 'BROWN OCHRE' CARTER 34 PANTONE 463 BS 4800 08 C 39 'BISON'	**2** 'VERMILION' CARTER 36 PANTONE 485 BS 5252 04 E 55 OR BS 381 536 'POPPY RED'	**3** 'CRIMSON LAKE' CARTER 28 PANTONE 188 BS 381 540 'CRIMSON'

North Eastern Railway

The constituents of the North Eastern Railway included some of the oldest railways in the world. Many of the lines built before 1850 were part of George Hudson's group of companies, including the York & North Midland, Great North of England and Newcastle & Darlington Junction railways, all opened between 1840 and 1844. The GNoE and N&DJ were amalgamated into the York & Newcastle Railway in 1846 and absorbed the Newcastle & Berwick Railway in 1847 to form the York, Newcastle & Berwick.

The local rival to the Hudson group was the Leeds Northern Railway, opened as the Leeds & Thirsk in 1849, renamed in 1851 and extended to Stockton in 1852. Ruinous competition ensued and, after a meeting of the three protagonists, amalgamation was seen as the only way out. The North Eastern Railway came into being in 1854.

The Newcastle & Carlisle Railway was absorbed in 1862, and the Stockton & Darlington Railway in 1863. The NER was then in the fortunate position of having virtually the entire district to itself. The railway had an excellent reputation with the travelling public, running good local expresses as well as the more prestigious trains. It also had the heaviest coal and mineral traffic of any British railway. Its length in 1908 was 1,698 miles. The NER became a constituent of the London & North Eastern Railway in 1923, and passed into the North Eastern Region of British Railways in 1948. Ten years later, this region was combined with the Eastern Region.

The Locomotive Superintendents of the NER were Mr Edward Fletcher (1854-83), Mr Alexander McDonnell (1883-84), Mr Thomas Wordsell (1885-90), Mr Wilson Wordsell (1890-1910) and Mr (later Sir) Vincent Raven (1910-23).

Before 1885 there was no standardisation, the former workshops of the constituents (Gateshead, Darlington, York and Leeds) being given a free hand, although all schemes were based on light green. It was on the appointment of Thomas Wordsell in 1885 that a system-wide standard livery was seen. The main body colour was light chrome green [1], and frames and valances were a rich red-brown, almost crimson lake. Tanks, tenders, splashers and cabs were bordered with a wide band of the red-brown lake. Between the two colours was a band of black, lined on the inside with white, and on the outside with vermilion [2]. Boiler bands were black, lined white. The red-brown valances were edged black, fine-lined vermilion. On

Wilson Wordsell Class 'R1' 4-4-0 No. 1238, built at Darlington in 1909, illustrates the simple dignity of the North Eastern livery. The artist (one of several working under the name of F. Moore), using a works grey photograph, has depicted the engine as if it were carrying the gold lining, which is not thought to be the case.
Author's collection

tenders and tanksides appeared the letters "N. E. R." with full stops, in gold block letters, shaded in red, brown and black.

New numberplates were introduced, being elliptical with central numerals. Over the number in very small letters was "NORTH EASTERN RAILWAY" and underneath was the place and date of construction. All characters were polished brass on a black background. Safety valve covers and cleading between the smokebox and boiler were polished brass.

From about 1888, the passenger tender locomotives carried a new lettering style. This included the first armorial device, consisting of a triangular arrangement of the shields of the three constituents surrounded by a circular garter carrying "NORTH EASTERN RAILWAY". The new lettering was "NORTH [device] EASTERN" in small sans-serif gold lettering, shaded in the standard way. Other engines retained the usual "N.E.R." initials.

On the retirement of Thomas Wordsell in 1890, he was succeeded

Thomas Wordsell locomotive livery 1885-90.

by his younger brother Wilson Wordsell. Changes soon became apparent in the livery. The general style was maintained but the red-brown edging and framing was abandoned. Body panels were now edged with black and fine-lined white, and all lining above the footplate was in bands of black, fine-lined white. The valances and frames were now black, lined with vermilion. Wheels were green, with black tyres and axle ends, both fine-lined white. Safety valve covers were polished brass, and some classes of engine had brass chimney caps. Bufferbeams were vermilion, edged in black and fine-lined white, although goods engines had plain vermilion. The number appeared thereon in the usual form: "Nº [hook] 1877", for example, in large gold characters shaded to right and below in dark blue, light blue and white. For a short time around 1900, several engines appeared with the number only, positioned to the left of the drawhook.

From the end of 1899 a second armorial device was adopted, which was much more elaborate. It no longer had a garter but was surrounded by filigree work and had the name as a motto below. This device appeared henceforth on tenders carrying the full

lettering, and at the same time the tender lettering also increased in size. The first device still appeared on the driving wheel splashers of the large express engines then appearing and the 4-2-2 'Singles'.

A number of the larger express passenger engines – the Class 'S' and Class 'S1' 4-6-0s, and Class 'V' 4-4-2s – were given a special treatment. White remained on most of the lining, but on the black lining panels on cabs and tenders, the inner fine-lining was replaced by a ¼-inch band of gold. While boiler bands remained edged with white, a ⅜-inch gold line was added to each side on the boiler cleading. The usual white lining on the bufferbeams was also replaced by gold.

From June 1904 black was adopted for goods engines, a single ¼-inch vermilion line following the edges of tender panels, tanksides, cabs, splashers, valances and steps, and on each edge of the boiler bands. Coupling and connecting rods were vermilion, but brass fitments remained polished. Lettering was the standard "N.E.R.", but the Class 'X' 4-8-0T hump shunters of 1909 were unusual in that they were black yet carried the full passenger-type lettering on the tanksides.

Also from 1904, the locomotive class in 1½-inch white characters appeared on the lower edge of bufferbeams, for example "CLASS [hook] V1". On those engines that received the special 'gold' lining, these characters were also gold.

Mr (later Sir) Vincent Raven, who had been Chief Assistant for many years, succeeded Mr Wordsell in 1910. There were few changes in the engine livery, except that the full lettering appeared on the new black-painted Class 'Y' 4-6-2 tank engines. A special black livery was also adopted in 1912 for the Classes 'S', 'S1' and 'S2' 4-6-0s, which were increasingly being used for fast goods working. The standard single line of vermilion was supplemented by an inner line of gold on tenders, cabsides, splashers and cylinders. Boiler bands had an outer band of gold on the cleading. The full "NORTH [device] EASTERN" lettering was applied to the tenders.

From March 1917 all goods and mineral engines (including the 4-6-0s) were painted unlined black as they went through shops. Furthermore, a new method of displaying the number was adopted for train control purposes. The old large brass numberplates were

replaced by very small ones, the engines now carried their numbers in large 12-inch numerals on the tenders or tanksides, and "R" was omitted from the 6-inch initials, for example "N. 2259 E.".

From 1919, vermilion lining was restored to the black engines but the large train control numbers were maintained. By 1922, when the prototype express electric locomotive No. 13 and the first two of the Pacific 4-6-2s were completed, the large numberplates had returned and the train control numbers had been abandoned.

The NER bequeathed its locomotive livery style to the new London & North Eastern Railway, albeit with the Great Northern Railway green supplanting the NER green. The simple style suited large engines very well, illustrated by comparing the two railways' Pacific classes, which appeared almost simultaneously. The GNR green and brown scheme looks too fussy and old-fashioned to suit the first engine, Class 'A1' No. 1470 *Great Northern*, but the green and black of NER Class '4-6-2' No. 2400 (later *City of Newcastle*) looks more dignified and modern.

In Mr Fletcher's time, carriage painting was a plum colour for First

and Second Class coaches, with dark green for Thirds and Brakes. From 1885 all carriages were being painted crimson lake [3]. It is remarked how bright and yet deep the colour was when first applied, and how it then weathered to a shade almost indistinguishable from the Midland's carriages; this suggests to me that carmine was used as the top glazing coat, which has fugitive tones that fade over time. Lining was in yellow around all panels of beading, with a vermilion fine-line on the outer edge. Until 1899 the brake ends of carriages were vermilion. Mansell wheel centres were crimson with black ironwork and white tyres. Solebars were crimson with a panel of vermilion of just over half their depth, outlined in yellow. This panel had been abandoned by 1905. Droplights were varnished wood. Roofs were generally white, but when clerestory carriages appeared in 1895, only their top roofs were white; clerestory sides and the roof down to eaves level were crimson. Clerestories were lined in vermilion only.

Until 1899 lettering was in sans-serif gold characters, shaded to right and below in red and brown with white highlights. The 4-inch initials "N.E.R." with full stops were placed to the left and the

number to the right of carriages in the waist, with the first device usually central. Class marking was in words.

From 1899 a new style appeared. This was in gold seriffed characters, shaded to left and below with red and pink, and shadowed to right and below in black and brown. On 6-wheel stock the old lettering arrangement was retained, but on the new clerestory bogie coaches the words "NORTH EASTERN RAILWAY" were placed in the eaves panels, with two numbers in the waist and devices below, although there were many variations. Where glass toplights precluded the use of eaves lettering on some designs of bogie vehicles, the initials were again used, except for the new matchsided stock, which retained the name in full along the lower panels of the body.

Non-passenger carriage stock was painted crimson lake, sometimes lined out similarly to the passenger vehicles, but lettered in yellow, shaded in red and brown. This stock never received the seriffed lettering.

There were so many different types of wagon that only generalities can be considered here. It was from 1892 that standardised white

N.E.R   20045

6~7~0

NIGEL J.L.DIGBY 2002

lettering was introduced on a medium grey, with black below the solebar. The standard numberplate was rectangular, 13 x 7 inches with incurved corners, and carried the number centrally flanked by "NORTH" above and "EASTERN" below. During the years 1896-1903, stock was turned out in a light grey. Thereafter medium grey was restored, until from about 1919 a darker grey was used.

The standard lettering was "N.E.R." (with full stops) to the left and the number to the right. This was placed on the lower plank of general open wagons, but on the upper planks of covered wagons. There were numerous examples of the initials being larger in size than the numbers, and numbers were often followed by a full stop too. On the 1896-1903 light grey livery, the white characters were heavily shaded with black. From 1911, the large initials "N E" were introduced, being 12 inches square.

Goods brake vans were brown oxide [4], with vermilion ends, white roofs and yellow lettering. The lettering was small but plentiful, and besides the usual "N.E.R" and number also indicated the Division of the railway to which it belonged (Northern, Central

or Southern), if the van was for the exclusive use of the Mineral Department, and its home station. From 1905, brakes were painted Indian red [5], again with vermilion ends. Lettering was now white, and slightly simplified, omitting the division. Finally, the introduction of the large letters in 1911 saw the omission of most extraneous lettering, but the home station still featured on most vans.

Refrigerator vans were white, with black letters shaded red. Gunpowder vans were vermilion with white letters. From 1905 goods vehicles fitted with automatic brakes and complying with passenger train requirements were painted Indian red. Formerly, they are believed to have been crimson lake.

Wagon sheets carried the initials "N.E.R." in large stencilled seriffed characters on each long side, with the number below in the same size. The number was also stencilled in a smaller size at each short side. On the back (or inside) of the sheet, the number appeared again in very small numerals on each side, and there was a small X at each corner.

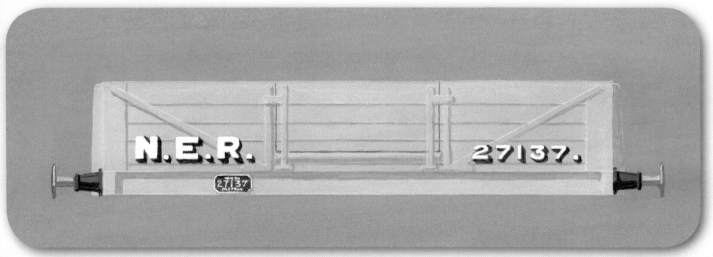

Light grey goods livery 1896-1903.

Brake van with lettering used from 1911.

Wilson Wordsell Class 'V/09' 4-4-2 No. 698, built at Darlington in 1910, at Wiske Moor water troughs on a Newcastle to Liverpool express working. The train is a seven-coach set of the 1908 toplight vestibuled stock, including a 12-wheeled dining car (third vehicle).   *Author's collection*

1 'LIGHT GREEN'
CARTER 7
PANTONE 364
BS 381 218
'GRASS GREEN'

2 'VERMILION'
CARTER 36
PANTONE 485
BS 5252 04 E 55
OR BS 381 536
'POPPY RED'

3 'CRIMSON LAKE'
CARTER 28
PANTONE 188
BS 381 540 'CRIMSON'

4 'OXIDE BROWN'
CARTER 29
PANTONE 483
BS 381 448
'DEEP INDIAN RED'

5 'INDIAN RED'
CARTER 31
PANTONE 181
BS 4800 04 C 39
'COPPER BEECH'